Wilderness Visitors, Experiences, and Management Preferences:

How They Vary With Use Level and Length of Stay

David N. Cole

Troy E. Hall

United States Department of Agriculture / Forest Service

Rocky Mountain Research Station

Research Paper RMRS-RP-71

July 2008

Cole, David N.; Hall, Troy E. 2008. **Wilderness Visitors, Experiences, and Management Preferences: How They Vary With Use Level and Length of Stay.** Res. Pap. RMRS-RP-71. Fort Collins, CO: U.S. Department of Agriculture, Forest Service, Rocky Mountain Research Station. 61 p.

Abstract

We explore the extent to which visitor experiences and management preferences vary between the most heavily used places in wilderness and places that are less popular. We also contrast day and overnight users. The study was conducted in Forest Service administered wildernesses in Oregon and Washington using both on-site and mailback questionnaires. The on-site questionnaires were administered as visitors exited the wilderness at 36 trailheads in 13 wildernesses. The trail use ranged from very high to moderate. To include visitors who selected low use trails, we sent mailback questionnaires to self-issue permit holders. We describe visitor characteristics, trip characteristics, motivations and experiences, encounters with other groups, attitudes toward recreation management, and opinions about the Forest Service. Differences related to use level were surprisingly small. Differences between day and overnight users were also small. We found evidence that wilderness experiences were adversely affected at high use locations but most visitors consider these effects to be of little importance. Most visitors to the more popular places make psychological adjustments to heavy use, allowing most of them to find solitude and have what they consider "a real wilderness experience." Consequently, most are not supportive of use limits to avoid people-related problems. We draw conclusions about potential indicators, standards, and management actions for heavily-used places in wilderness.

Keywords: management preferences, recreation experiences, day use, visitor management, visitor surveys, wilderness recreation

Authors

David N. Cole is Research Geographer with the Aldo Leopold Wilderness Research Institute, Missoula, MT. He received an A.B. in geography from the University of California, Berkeley, and a Ph.D. in geography from the University of Oregon.

Troy E. Hall is Associate Professor in the Department of Conservation Social Sciences at the University of Idaho, Moscow, ID. She received a B.A. in anthropology from Pomona College, an M.A. in anthropology from Duke University and a Ph.D. in forestry from Oregon State University.

Ackowledgments

This research was supported by funds from the Aldo Leopold Wilderness Research Institute, Rocky Mountain Research Station, the Pacific Northwest Region of the Forest Service, and the University of Idaho. We appreciate the help of numerous field assistants and the review comments of Susan Sater, Rudy King, Steve Martin, and Lisa Therrell.

Contents

Introduction	1
Study Design	1
Trailhead Surveys	2
Mailback Questionnaires	3
Data Analysis and Interpretation	4
Results and Discussion	4
Visitor Characteristics	4
Trip Characteristics	8
Motivations and Experiences	10
Encounters with Other Groups	15
Attitudes Toward Management of Recreation in Wilderness	24
Opinions About the Forest Service	32
Summary and Management Implications	32
Differences Related to Amount of Use	33
Differences Between Day and Overnight Users	35
Methodological Implications	36
Indicators and Standards	36
Appropriate Management Actions	38
References	39
Appendix A: Trailhead Exit Questionnaire Version 1	41
Appendix B: Questions Asked on the Other Three Versions of the Trailhead Exit Questionnaires But Not on Version 1	47
Appendix C: Mailback Questionnaire	54
Appendix D: Questions on Other Version of Mailback Questionnaire Not on Version One	60

Introduction

Wilderness use, particularly in urban-proximate western wildernesses, is increasing, and a large part of this growth comes from day use (Chavez 2000). There is considerable controversy about appropriate management of popular wilderness trails and destinations generally and about day use specifically. Much of the controversy stems from varied interpretations of the language from the 1964 Wilderness Act that describes what wilderness should offer visitors: "outstanding opportunities for solitude or a primitive and unconfined type of recreation." There is growing debate regarding what causes more degradation of solitude or primitive and unconfined recreation: growing crowds of visitors or Forest Service imposed use limits and restrictions, especially limits on day use (Spring 2001; Worf 2001). In Oregon and Washington, this controversy has led to administrative reversals of direction and successful appeals of Forest Service plans. In other regions it has led to litigation. The controversy largely results from a lack of consensus among legitimate wilderness stakeholders about how to balance the benefits of public access with concern for maintaining outstanding opportunities for the types of experience wilderness is supposed to provide.

Controversy is inevitable, given the disparate views of wilderness stakeholders (Seekamp and others 2006). However, the intensity of the controversy is aggravated by inconsistent decision-making and by the lack of an adequate informational basis (science and monitoring data) for decision-making. Tough, value-laden decisions must be made about appropriate management objectives (including indicators and standards) regarding experiential conditions in wilderness and about the management actions needed to keep conditions in compliance with standards. Scientific information is needed, not because it will identify "the right decisions" or even make decisions easier, but because it will make decisions more informed. Scientific information will make it easier to explain and justify decisions, because the likely consequences of a given decision or alternatives to it will have been explored and can be articulated.

Recently, managerial effectiveness has been challenged on several fronts regarding the provision of opportunities for appropriate experiences in wilderness. First, visitors and researchers have both questioned whether the types of indicators that have been selected for experience quality (usually measures of encounters between groups) indeed indicate what they are designed to indicate (Glaspell and others 2003). Some question whether encounters is an adequate proxy for "outstanding opportunities for solitude" or for "primitive and unconfined" experiences (Watson and Roggenbuck 1997). Apart from whether the indicator itself is appropriate is the question of whether the particular standards selected (usually on the order of 10 encounters per day in the most popular places) are appropriate.

Other basic questions about experiences have arisen. Assuming that wildernesses should provide unique "wilderness" experiences, some people have asserted that certain visitors (for example, day users) do not seek "wilderness experiences," while other types of visitors (for example, overnight users or purists) do seek them (Papenfuse and others 2000). Some people assert that visitors cannot have "wilderness experiences" in high-density areas. Proponents of these assertions often argue that managers should restrict use to provide the experiences sought by those who seek truly "wilderness" types of experiences (Haas and Wells 2000). These assertions are underlain by numerous untested assumptions, however, about the experiences sought by different visitor types and attained in different settings (Hall 2001).

Given the need for active management of heavy use and day use in wilderness and the high degree of controversy and public scrutiny of wilderness management, we undertook studies of visitors to a number of Forest Service administered wildernesses in Oregon and Washington. We studied visitors in places that varied widely in amount of use, as well as visitors on day and overnight trips. The primary purposes of our research were to (1) understand the nature of visitor experiences in high-use wilderness and the influence of use levels on experience and (2) provide information helpful in identifying appropriate indicators and standards related to experiences and evaluating the desirability of various management actions, including use limitation. Therefore, particular attention is focused on encounters with other visitors, the effects of those encounters, opinions about appropriate encounter levels, and opinions about techniques for managing crowded conditions.

Study Design

We wanted to study visitors to the most popular Forest Service administered wilderness locations in Oregon and Washington and compare them to visitors in less popular locations. We were also interested in studying as broad a range as possible of wildernesses in Oregon and Washington. Because amount of use varies more among trails within a wilderness than among entire wildernesses, we attempted to obtain representative samples of visitors to specific trailheads rather than entire wildernesses. Consequently, our goal was to survey exiting visitors from as many of the most popular trailheads in Oregon and Washington as possible, along with nearby less popular trailheads. For reasons of efficiency, we could only conduct trailhead exit surveys at trailheads that received at least moderate amounts of use. Consequently, we supplemented trailhead surveys with mailback surveys, a more efficient procedure for surveying visitors to low use trailheads.

Trailhead Surveys

Our initial strategy was to find two moderate and one high use trailhead close to each other. Each group of trailheads was to be sampled twice during the summer season of 2003 (generally late June to early September), each sample over a 9-day block of time. High use trailheads would be sampled on two weekend days and three weekdays during that block. Each of the two moderate use trailheads would be sampled on three weekend days and three to four weekdays. Within these constraints, assignment was random. High use trails, then, were to be sampled a total of 10 days, distributed across weekdays and weekends in two noncontiguous time blocks. Moderate use trails were to be sampled a total of 13 days, distributed across weekdays and weekends, in two noncontiguous time blocks. In reality, we could not always find trailheads in close proximity that matched our criteria and were forced to adapt our procedures.

Ultimately, we collected data from 36 trailheads in 13 wildernesses in Oregon and Washington. These trailheads were placed in three categories based on use levels ascertained from the number of visitors counted on sample days and the number of annual permits issued. We classified nine trailheads as "very high" use because we observed an average of more than 20 groups per day and found more than 1,500 permits per year were issued for these trails. At the nine "high" use trailheads, we observed 11 to 20 groups per day and found 550 to 1,500 permits per year issued. At the 18 "moderate" use trailheads, we observed fewer than 10 groups per day or fewer than 500 permits per year issued. Generally from north to south, these wildernesses and trailheads were:

1. Mount Baker Wilderness
    a. Yellow Aster Butte (Trail 699) (High Use)
    b. Hannegan Pass (Trail 674) (High Use)

2. Alpine Lakes Wilderness
    a. Pratt Lake (Trail 1007) (Very High Use)
    b. Snow Lake (Trail 1013) (Very High Use)
    c. Gold Creek (Trail 1314) (Moderate Use)
    d. Paddy-Go-Easy Pass (Trail 1595A) (Moderate Use)
    e. Waptus River (Trail 1310) (Moderate Use)
    f. Tucquala Campground (Trails 1345 and 1376) (Moderate Use)

3. Norse Peak Wilderness
    a. Norse Peak (Trail 1191) (Moderate Use)
    b. Union Creek (Trail 956) (Moderate Use)
    c. Crow Lake Way (Trail 953) (Moderate Use)

4. William O. Douglas Wilderness
    a. Dewey Lake (Pacific Crest Trail) (High Use)

5. Goat Rocks Wilderness
    a. Snowgrass Flats (Trail 96) (Moderate Use)
    b. Walupt Lake (Trails 98 and 101) (Moderate Use)

6. Mount Adams Wilderness
    a. Killen Creek (Trail 113) (Moderate Use)
    b. Cold Springs, South Climb of Mt. Adams (Trail 183) (Very High Use)

7. Indian Heaven Wilderness
    a. Indian Heaven, Cultus Creek Campground (Trail 33) (Moderate Use)

8. Mark O. Hatfield Wilderness
    a. Eagle Creek (Very High Use)
    b. Wahtum Lake (Moderate Use)

9. Mount Hood Wilderness
    a. Cloud Cap (Very High Use)
    b. Vista Ridge (Moderate Use)
    c. Top Spur (High Use)
    d. Burnt Lake (High Use)
    e. Ramona Falls (Very High Use)
    f. Timberline (Very High Use)
    g. Elk Meadows (Moderate Use)

10. Salmon-Huckleberry Wilderness
    a. Salmon River (High Use)
    b. Salmon Butte (Moderate Use)

11. Eagle Cap Wilderness
    a. Two Pan (Trails 1662 and 1670) (High Use)
    b. Wallowa Lake (Trails 1804 and 1820) (Very High Use)

12. Mount Jefferson Wilderness
    a. Jack Lake (High Use)
    b. Cabot Lake (Moderate Use)

13. Three Sisters Wilderness
    a. Devil's Lake, South Sister Climb (Very High Use)
    b. Elk Lake (Trail 3515) (Moderate Use)
    c. Six Lakes (Trail 3526) (Moderate Use)
    d. Lucky Lake (Moderate Use)

Researchers were present at trailheads for at least 6 hours per day (usually 8 hours), with sampling times adjusted to match the times of day that people were likely to be present. There were a total of 453 sampling days, distributed such that 27 of the 36 trailheads were sampled at least 10 days. The other nine trailheads were sampled less than 10 days. Researchers attempted to contact all adult (16 years and older) members of all groups, both day and overnight visitors, and asked them to participate as they exited the wilderness. About 70 percent of the sample consisted of people surveyed on weekend/holiday days, despite the fact that there were more weekday sample days. About 67 percent of the sample consisted of day users. This proportion should provide a reasonable estimate of the percent of visits at these trailheads that are day visits, since day and overnight users were equally likely to be sampled and there was little difference in refusal rates between day and overnight users.

In all, about 12,000 adult visitors (16 years or greater) exited from the trailheads on the days when sampling was being conducted—7,860 (65 percent) of these visitors were asked to fill out a questionnaire on-site. It was not possible to contact everyone at high use trails and on busy days, but researchers attempted to document all visitors entering or exiting the trailhead. Seventy-two percent of those asked agreed to fill out a questionnaire, providing a sample size of 5,712 completed questionnaires. Most of the visitors that were contacted were hikers. Equestrians accounted for less than 2 percent of the sample. Although only 8 percent of the sample consisted of mountaineers, most visitors at two of the very high use trailheads (Cold Springs and Devil's Lake) were climbing a mountain nearby (Mt. Adams and South Sister, respectively).

Two fundamentally different questionnaires were administered at trailheads. One focused on the trips people took, what they experienced, and how they evaluated their experience. The second focused on opinions about management. Additionally, two slightly different versions of each questionnaire were developed to allow for slight variations on several questions. Consequently, there were four different instruments, each of which was given in approximately equal numbers at each trailhead by systematically rotating the distribution. We had a sample size of at least 1,400 for each question and substantially more for questions that were repeated on different versions. This provided a sufficient sample for analysis when results were subdivided by trailhead use level and by length of stay.

Mailback Questionnaires

We used mailback questionnaires to include the opinions of visitors to low use trailheads. Many wilderness managers in Oregon and Washington require visitors to complete a self-issued wilderness permit at the trailhead at the beginning of their trip. We were able to obtain the 2002 permits for the following 19 wildernesses (out of 59 Forest Service administered wildernesses in the two states) as the sample frame for this study: Diamond Peak, Eagle Cap, Glacier View, Goat Rocks, Indian Heaven, Mark O. Hatfield, Mt. Adams, Mt. Hood, Mt. Jefferson, Mt. Washington, Norse Peak, Opal Creek, Pasayten, Salmon-Huckleberry, Tatoosh, Three Sisters, Trapper Creek, Waldo Lake, and William O. Douglas. For the Salmon-Huckleberry and Mark O. Hatfield Wildernesses, permits were collected only at selected popular trailheads, so visitors to other trails in these wildernesses were not represented in our study.

It is important to note that not all visitors comply with the requirement of obtaining a permit. Moreover, group leaders are more likely to fill out the permit, and leaders may be more experienced than other group members. Therefore, the sampling frame represents only people who filled out permits, not all visitors. Since this sample is not strictly comparable to the trailhead survey sample, we sent mailback questionnaires to a representative sample of visitors to all trails, as well as to a sample of visitors to the low use trails.

A one-in-30 systematic sample drawn from all permits generated a database of 1,637 names for the representative sample of all trails. The sample included day and overnight hikers, climbers, and stock users in proportion to their representation in the population. Approximately 9 percent of the names on this list visited trails we defined as low use trails. Low use trailheads were those at which fewer than 100 permits had been completed in 2002. To generate the sample of visitors from low use trails, a one-in-12 systematic sample was drawn from permits issued to visitors to low use trails. This generated an additional 444 names.

Following Dillman's method (Salant & Dillman 1994), a reminder postcard was sent out ten days following the initial mailing. Approximately 10 days after the reminder postcard, a second survey was sent to the remaining non-respondents. Of the 344 surveys sent to people in the low use sample with valid addresses, 239 (70 percent) were completed and returned. Of the 1,287 surveys sent to the representative sample of all wilderness visitors with valid addresses, 814 (63 percent) were completed and returned. No non-response checks were performed.

Two different questionnaires were administered to the low use sample and the sample of all users. Having two versions allowed us to include a broader range of questions while keeping the response burden to a reasonable level. The included questions were taken from those that were asked in the trailhead survey. However, because respondents in this mailback study could not be asked about a specific wilderness trip, questions specific to a particular place or trip were not included. Across all trailheads, about 500 questionnaires of each type were completed. About one-third of the questions were common to both questionnaires, while two-thirds were asked on only one instrument. Consequently we had a sample size of at least 500 for all questions. However, in cases where questions were asked on only one instrument, the sample size for low-use visitors was closer to 100.

Data Analysis and Interpretation

Our primary use of statistical inference was to test for differences among visitors related to the use level of the trail they had selected. Results of the trailhead surveys and mailback questionnaires must be analyzed separately. The trailhead survey dataset had three levels of use: very high, high, and moderate, while the mailback questionnaire dataset compared low-use trail visitors to the entire population of visitors. In both cases, we considered use level to be an ordinal scale variable. We also assessed differences between day and overnight users based on the trailhead survey data. Where the dependent variables were nominal, we used Pearson's chi-square; where they were ordinal, we used Somers d. Where the dependent variable was interval, we usually report means and standard errors and used analysis of variance and t tests. For a few highly skewed variables, we report medians and used Kruskal-Wallis and Mann-Whitney tests. For both analyses of variance and Kruskal-Wallis tests, we used Tukey-based multiple comparisons to draw conclusions about differences between factor levels. For a few experiential variables we conducted stepwise multiple regression analyses to understand the effects of use, using two estimates of encounter rates—the number of groups encountered that day and the percent of time in sight of other groups—as independent variables.

Given the large sample size we often had, small differences can be statistically significant. The reader is reminded that statistical significance merely relates to how confident we are that an observed difference among samples is a real difference among populations. Readers are encouraged to draw their own conclusions about magnitude of effect. Generally, we refer to differences smaller than about 10 percent as small differences. Given the large sample for most questions, there were few situations where there were large observed differences that were not statistically significant.

It is also interesting, for some questions, to ponder the differences between responses to the trailhead surveys and the responses of all visitors to the mailback questionnaire. In some cases, differences seem reasonable in light of likely differences between the group members that are more or less likely to fill out the permit. In other cases, however, differences are of a magnitude or direction that suggests they reflect when the survey was taken—immediately after hiking out or months after the trip.

Results and Discussion

Visitor Characteristics

Few questions were asked regarding visitor sociodemographics because these characteristics tend to be relatively stable from wilderness to wilderness and substantial information of this type has already been collected elsewhere (Hendee and Dawson 2002). Visitors at very high use trailheads were slightly younger, on average, than visitors to less popular trailheads, but the relative proportion of males and females did not vary with use level (table 1). The age and gender differences between respondents in the trailhead and mailback surveys (table 1) provide one example of differences between group leaders and group members. Older males are more likely than other group members to fill out the permit. Differences between day and overnight visitors are much more pronounced; day visitors are typically somewhat older and more likely to be female (table 2).

Distance Traveled to Trailheads

We asked visitors how far they traveled from home to the trailhead. Although one-quarter of visitors lived within an hour's drive of the trailhead and one-half lived within a 2-hour drive, 10 percent of visitors lived at least a day from the trailhead. Median distance from home to trail decreased as use of the trail increased,

Table 1. Age (mean; standard error) and gender; use level variation.

	Very high n = 2551	High n = 1593	Moderate n = 1217	All visitors n = 809	Low use n = 238
Mean age (of those over 16 years)	**38**(0.3)[a]	**41**(0.4)[b]	**40**(0.4)[b]	48(0.7)	49(0.4)
Percent female	41	45	42	27	25

Bold values with different superscripts are significantly different from one another (p ≤ 0.05).

Table 2. Age (mean; standard error) and gender; day and overnight users.

	Day n = 3584	Overnight n = 1705
Mean age (of those over 16 years)	**41**(0.2)	**36**(0.3)
Percent female	**46**	**36**

Bold values are significantly different from one another (p ≤ 0.05).

while mean distance increased (table 3). Very high use trailheads were used more than moderately used trailheads by people living close by, but they were also used more by people who live far away. This likely reflects the proximity of these trailheads to large metropolitan areas served by airports, which provide easier access to visitors from distant places. Or, these trailheads are places to take visitors from out of town. Median distance traveled was less for day users than for overnight users, but mean distance traveled was similar (table 3). Day users were much more likely to live very close to trailheads. Forty-three percent of day users lived within 50 miles of the trailhead compared to only 17 percent of overnight users. However, day hikers were also more likely than overnight hikers to live far away.

Day Trips Versus Overnight Trips

Most wilderness visitors (77 percent) take day trips to wilderness more frequently than they take overnight trips. About 19 percent of visitors make only day visits to wilderness. Visitors to low use trailheads take proportionately more overnight trips compared to visitors to more popular trails (table 4).

Table 3. Distance traveled to trailhead.

Miles from trailhead	Very high	High	Moderate	Day	Overnight
median	**60**[a]	**75**[b]	**90**[b]	60	100
mean	**318**(16)[a]	**267**(16)[a]	**200**(14)[b]	277(12)	276(16)

Bold values and those with different superscripts are significantly different from one another (p ≤ 0.05); n = 1200 to 2482.

Table 4. Percent of wilderness trips that are day visits; use level variation.

	Very high	High	Moderate	All visitors	Low use
Wilderness trips that are day visits (percent)	71	70	64	**64**	**58**

Bold values are significantly different from one another (p ≤ 0.05); n = 232 to 2397.

Wilderness Experience and Attachment

We asked questions that tap into three dimensions of wilderness experience: experience with this particular wilderness, experience in varied wilderness areas, and frequency of wilderness visitation. Although only 3 percent of visitors were on their first wilderness trip, 43 percent were on their first visit to the "destination or area" where we contacted them. Contrary to our expectations, visitors to more popular trails had higher levels of wilderness experience compared to visitors to less popular trails. Repeat users were slightly more common at the more popular trailheads than at the moderate use ones (table 5). Frequency of wilderness visitation did not vary with use level but experience in varied wilderness areas increased as use level increased (table 6). Day users were also more experienced than were overnight visitors by these measures. They had visited the local wilderness more often, taken more frequent wilderness trips, and been to more individual wildernesses in their lifetime (tables 5 and 7).

We asked three questions intended to provide insight into how attached people are to wilderness (how important wilderness is in their lives). Responses could range from -3 (strongly disagree) to +3 (strongly agree). Most wilderness visitors were highly attached to wilderness (table 8). About one-half strongly agreed (+3 rating) with the statement "I get greater satisfaction out of visiting wilderness than other areas." However, wilderness attachment scores did not vary

Table 5. Local wilderness experience.

	Very high	High	Moderate	Day	Overnight
First-time visitors to this trailhead (percent)	40[a]	43[a]	49[b]	39	51

Bold values and those with different superscripts are significantly different (p ≤ 0.05); n = 1188 to 3450.

Table 6. Frequency of wilderness visitation and number of wildernesses visited; use level variation.

	Very high	High	Moderate	All visitors	Low use
Median wilderness visits/year	5	5	5	5	5
Median number of other wildernesses visited	10[a]	9[b]	9[b]	8	7

Bold values and those with different superscripts are significantly different from one another (Kruskal-Wallis, Mann-Whitney, p ≤ 0.05); n = 236 to 2435.

Table 7. Frequency of wilderness visitation and number of wildernesses visited; day and overnight users.

	Day	Overnight
Median wilderness visits/year	**6**	**4**
Median number of other wildernesses visited	**10**	**9**

Bold values are significantly different from one another (p ≤ 0.05); n = 1649 to 3438.

Table 8. Wilderness attachment scores (mean, standard error); use level variation.

Wilderness attachment item	Very high	High	Moderate	All visitors	Low use
Life organized around wilderness	0.8(.03)	0.8(.04)	0.9(.05)	0.7(.06)	0.9(.10)
Wilderness is a part of me	1.6(.03)	1.6(.03)	1.6(.04)	1.9(.04)	1.9(.08)
More satisfaction from wilderness	2.1(.03)	2.1(.03)	2.2(.03)	2.1(.04)	2.2(.07)

Scale: +3 (strongly agree) to -3 (strongly disagree). Scores did not differ significantly with use level (p ≤ 0.05); n = 233 to 2400.

Table 9. Wilderness attachment scores (mean, standard error); day and overnight users.

Wilderness attachment item	Day	Overnight
Life organized around wilderness	0.8(.03)	0.9(.04)
Wilderness is a part of me	**1.6(.02)**	**1.7(.03)**
More satisfaction from wilderness	2.1(.02)	2.2(.03)

Scale: +3 (strongly agree) to -3 (strongly disagree). **Bold** values are significantly different from one another ($p \leq 0.05$); n = 1639 to 3403.

significantly with use level or length of stay (table 8). The only statistically significant difference related to length of stay was that overnight users agreed more strongly than day users with the statement "I feel like wilderness is a part of me" (table 9). Measured on a 7-point scale, however, a difference of 0.1 seems negligible.

Interest in Wilderness Management

Most visitors reported being very interested in, and concerned about, the way the wilderness they had just visited was managed (table 10). Personal interest did not vary significantly with either use level or between day and overnight visitors (data not shown). Self-reported knowledge about wilderness was not as high as interest in wilderness management. Most people reported that they know a little bit about the legal definition of wilderness (table 11). Permit holders' self-reported knowledge about the legal definition of wilderness was much higher than that of the average visitor. Visitors to very high use trailheads were less knowledgeable compared to visitors to less popular trailheads and low use visitors were more knowledgeable than all users. Differences were small, however. Day users were also slightly less knowledgeable than overnight users (table 12).

Table 10. Importance of wilderness management (n = 2809).

How important to you personally is the way this area is managed?	Percent
I don't know	2
Not at all—I've never really thought about it	3
Not very—I haven't given it much thought and am not very concerned	3
Somewhat—I haven't thought a lot about it, but it seems important	34
Very—I think about it sometimes and have some concerns	41
Extremely—I think about it a lot and am very concerned	18

Table 11. Knowledge about wilderness; use level variation.

Knowledge of the Wilderness Act	Very high	High	Moderate	All visitors	Low use
	Percent				
Didn't know there was a land classification of wilderness	10	7	8	1	0
Have heard about wilderness but don't know anything about definition	26	22	25	11	6
Know a bit about what legal wilderness is	43	50	48	51	52
Know a lot about what legal wilderness is	20	21	20	37	42

Knowledge varied significantly among use levels as well as between low use and all visitors ($p \leq 0.05$). n = 235-2526.

Table 12. Knowledge about wilderness; day and overnight users.

Knowledge of the Wilderness Act	Day	Overnight
Didn't know there was a land classification of wilderness	9	8
Have heard about wilderness but don't know anything about definition	26	23
Know a bit about what legal wilderness is	46	47
Know a lot about what legal wilderness is	20	22

Knowledge varied significantly between day and overnight visitors ($p \leq 0.05$). n = 1705-3554.

Trip Characteristics

Trip Length

Questions about trip characteristics were not asked on the mailback questionnaires because respondents were surveyed up to a year after their trip. Therefore, only variation among trails receiving at least moderate use could be assessed. Day users were more common than overnight users at 27 of the 36 trailheads. Overall, 75 percent of people were on day trips. Although the length of the median day trip was just under 4 hours, 13 percent of trips exceeded 8 hours. Most overnight trips were short. One-night trips were most common, and only 9 percent of trips lasted for more than three nights. Day users made up a more substantial proportion of users as trailhead use level increased (table 13). Since day users were much more common on very high use trails, it is possible that some of the difference between very high use and other trails results more from the greater proportion of day users on those trails than from their heavier use. Surprisingly, trip lengths for both day and overnight visits increased as trailhead use level increased. Differences were small, however, and in the case of overnight trips, perhaps a result of chance (that is, the difference was not statistically significant).

Group Size

Most groups were small; the most common group size was two. Solo hikers made up 20 percent of groups, but only 7 percent of people were by themselves. Only 2 percent of groups had more than 10 people, but 9 percent of people came in groups larger than 10. Group size did not vary significantly with amount of use (table 14). Although mean group size did not differ significantly between overnight and day users, day users were more likely than overnight users to be hiking alone. The proportion of groups that were hiking, on horseback, or climbing did not vary significantly with amount of use (table 15). Only a few of the trailheads had significant proportions of equestrians or climbers and trailheads popular with these users spanned the use categories. Climbers made up a significantly larger proportion of overnight users than

Table 13. Trip length; use level variation.

	Very high	High	Moderate
Day users (% of people)	**84**[a]	**70**[b]	**66**[b]
Mean day trip length (hours)	**4.6**(.05)[a]	**4.4**(.06)[ab]	**4.3**(.07)[b]
Mean overnight trip length (nights)	2.7(0.3)	2.3(0.2)	2.0(0.1)

Bold values and those with different superscripts are significantly different ($p \leq 0.05$). n = 503-2694.

Table 14. Group size.

	Very high	High	Moderate	Day	Overnight
Mean group size (people)	2.7(.03)	2.7(.05)	2.6(.04)	2.7(.02)	2.7(.05)
Solo hikers (percent of groups)	18	20	17	**19**	**15**
Group size > 10 (percent of groups)	2	2	2	2	2

Bold values are significantly different ($p \leq 0.05$). n = 1590-5977

Table 15. Type of group.

	Very high	High	Moderate	Day	Overnight
Hikers (percent of groups)	91	97	90	93	87
Equestrians (percent of groups)	4	2	8	5	3
Climbers (percent of groups)	5	1	2	2	10

Type varied significantly between day and overnight users ($p \leq 0.05$). n = 1578-5967.

Table 16. Group size (mean; standard error), for different types of groups.

	Very high	High	Moderate	Day	Overnight
Hiker group size (people)	2.6(.03)	2.6(.05)	2.6(.04)	2.6(.02)	2.6(.05)
Equestrian group size (people)	5.5(.24)[a]	3.5(.26)[b]	3.0(.14)[b]	3.6(.16)	4.5(.21)
Climber group size (people)	2.9(.11)	4.3(.71)	2.6(.18)	3.0(.14)	2.6(.13)

Values with different superscripts are significantly different ($p \leq 0.05$). n = 1578-5967.

of day users. The mean group size of the different trip types did not vary much with either amount of use or length of stay (table 16). The only exception was the significantly larger size of equestrian groups at very high use trailheads (the only very high use trailhead with equestrian use was Wallowa Lake in the Eagle Cap Wilderness).

Registration Rates

Many of the trailheads where surveying took place had registration boxes that researchers could observe unobtrusively. At these trailheads, about two-thirds of entering groups registered. Registration rates were lower at the less popular trailheads (table 17). As has been found elsewhere, day users were less likely to register than overnight users.

Trip Experiences and Evaluations

Using an open-ended question, we asked users to describe the three high points and three low points of their trip. The most commonly mentioned trip high points were:

- scenic qualities (mentioned by 78 percent of respondents)
- water features (mentioned by 32 percent)
- solitude (mentioned by 13 percent)
- weather (mentioned by 13 percent)
- activities (mentioned by 12 percent)
- companions (mentioned by 10 percent)
- trail conditions (mentioned by 9 percent)
- peacefulness (mentioned by 8 percent)
- environmental diversity (mentioned by 7 percent)
- the climb (mentioned by 7 percent)

The most commonly mentioned low points were:

- bugs (mentioned by 19 percent)
- crowds (mentioned by 8 percent)
- dust (mentioned by 6 percent)
- horses (mentioned by 5 percent)
- trail conditions (mentioned by 5 percent)
- fatigue (mentioned by 5 percent)
- temperatures (mentioned by 5 percent)
- steep hiking (5 percent)

Nineteen percent of those who answered this question said that there were no low points. The percent of visitors who mentioned solitude as a high point exceeded the percent that mentioned crowds as a low point.

The proportion mentioning solitude as a high point was substantially higher at moderate use trailheads, but the very high use and high use trailheads did not differ (table 18). The percent mentioning crowding as a low point also increased as trailhead use level increased. In contrast, the percent using the word "wilderness" as a high point did not vary with use level, nor did the proportion who said there were no low points. Overnight users were more likely than day users to mention solitude and wilderness as high points. Day users were much more likely to say that there were no low points.

We asked people the extent to which what they experienced differed from what they had expected regarding the number of people they saw, evidence of impact from human use, and rules and regulations. Most visitors reported that what they encountered was close to what they expected. Visitors to moderate use trailheads were most likely to report that they saw fewer people than expected. At very high use

Table 17. Trailhead registration compliance.

	Very high	High	Moderate	Day	Overnight
Percent of groups that registered	**69**[a]	**70**[a]	**60**[b]	63	79

Bold values and those with different superscripts differed significantly ($p \leq 0.05$). n = 404-1781.

Table 18. Items mentioned as high or low points of the trip (percent of groups).

Percent reporting:	Very high	High	Moderate	Day	Overnight
Solitude was a high point	**11**[a]	**11**[a]	**21**[b]	11	19
Crowding was a low point	**10**[a]	**8**[a]	**4**[b]	7	9
Wilderness was a high point	3	3	3	2	5
No low points noted	20	20	16	**24**	**9**

Bold values and those with different superscripts differed significantly ($p \leq 0.05$). n = 591-1831.

Table 19. Relationship of expectations to what was experienced.

What was experienced in relation to what was expected regarding:	Very high	High	Moderate	Day	Overnight
The number of people seen	**0.0**(.04)[a]	**0.0**(.05)[a]	**-0.4**(.06)[b]	-0.1(.03)	0.0(.05)
Evidence of human impact	-0.2(.03)	-0.2(.05)	-0.2(.05)	**-0.2**(.03)	**-0.1**(.05)
Rules and regulations	-0.1(.03)	-0.2(.04)	-0.2(.04)	-0.2(.02)	-0.2(.04)

Scale: -3 (far less than expected) to +3 (far more than expected). **Bold** values and those with different superscripts are significantly different ($p \leq 0.05$). n = 584-1813.

trailheads, the average visitor reported that they expected to see the number of people that they actually saw (table 19). The relationship between what was expected and what was experienced regarding impacts and rules and regulations did not vary with use level. Differences between day and overnight visitors were also minimal.

We were interested in visitors' assessments of the severity of various potential problems. For this purpose, we asked people whether or not they noticed particular problems. If they did, we asked them to rate problem severity on a 7-point scale from "not at all" (1) to "slight" (3), "moderate" (5), and "big" (7). More than one-half of visitors (table 20) noticed most of the potential problems. Generally, more people noticed the biophysical impact problems than many of the social problems. Large groups and large numbers of day users were noticed by larger proportions of visitors in more heavily used places. For all problems, mean severity ratings were less than 3.0 (less than a slight problem). In addition to our finding that 20 to 50 percent of people did not notice these problems, we found most visitors did not view these problems as serious.

Biophysical impact problems were perceived to be somewhat more severe than social impact problems. The ratings for packstock impacts were notable given how few visitors used packstock. The only problem considered to be more severe in more popular places was the large numbers of day users. Problems with packstock impacts were judged to be more severe in moderate use areas. This might reflect the greater sensitivity of these visitors or the fact that stock users constituted 4 percent of the sample at moderate use trailheads and less than 1 percent of the sample at high use and very high use trailheads.

Overnight users noticed more problems than did day users (table 21). In some cases, this was because the problems were specific to camping, but it appears that day users were simply less attentive to many problems than overnight users. All problems were considered to be more severe by overnight users than by day users. This adds to the difference in proportion noticing problems. Overnight users experienced worse conditions and/or were less tolerant of what they experienced.

Motivations and Experiences

We were interested in learning about trip motivations—what people were hoping would happen on their wilderness visit in terms of what they would feel, sense, and experience. We were also interested in their evaluations of the extent to which these experiences were or were not achieved. We asked people about 14 different experiences, many of which are central to the wilderness concept (such as freedom, solitude, and remoteness). At trailheads, they were asked to rate how much they were **seeking it** (each of the 14 experiences) and how much they **experienced it**, both on 7-point scales from "not at all" to "very much." These results were in the context of the trip they had just completed. On the mailback questionnaire, the context was their entire history of wilderness trips. They were asked

Table 20. Evidence and severity of problems (mean; standard error); use level variation.

Problem	Percent who noticed			Mean problem severity		
	Very high	High	Moderate	Very high	High	Moderate
Trail wear and tear	78	78	79	2.8(.07)	2.9(.10)	2.9(.12)
Having to fill out permit/registration	79	74	75	1.8(.07)	1.9(.09)	1.8(.11)
Large numbers of day users	74[a]	69[ab]	63[a]	2.6(.07)[a]	2.7(.10)[a]	2.2(.11)[b]
Trampled areas from camping/walking	66	69	68	2.5(.08)	2.7(.10)	2.6(.12)
Trails that are poorly marked	66	63	66	2.4(.09)	2.4(.11)	2.6(.14)
Large groups	65[a]	63[a]	53[b]	2.3(.08)	2.4(.11)	2.1(.13)
Litter left behind by visitors	62	60	62	2.3(.09)	2.2(.12)	2.3(.13)
Uncontrolled dogs	63	61	60	2.0(.08)	2.2(.11)	2.1(.13)
Rules that restrict where people camp	54	57	54	2.1(09)	2.2(.11)	2.1(.12)
Inconsiderate behavior by others	58	54	53	2.1(.09)	2.3(.13)	2.1(.13)
Too many rules and regulations	55	54	52	1.9(.08)	1.8(.10)	2.1(.14)
Contact with ranger or volunteer	54	54	52	1.5(.06)	1.4(.07)	1.5(.09)
Impacts from recreational packstock	49[a]	55[ab]	59[b]	2.3(.11)[a]	2.5(.13)[a]	3.0(.16)[b]
Concern about your personal security	55	54	52	1.5(.06)	1.4(.07)	1.5(.09)
Noisy groups	**56**	**50**	**49**	2.4(.09)	2.6(.12)	2.3(.15)
Large numbers of overnight visitors	49	51	53	1.9(.08)	2.2(.12)	2.0(.12)
Human waste	49	50	49	2.0(.09)	1.9(.12)	2.0(.15)
Rules/regs not adequately enforced	49	49	48	1.9(.09)	2.2(.13)	2.0(.13)
Organized groups or outfitted parties	48	48	47	1.7(.07)	1.8(.10)	1.6(.10)

Scale for problem severity from 1 (not at all a problem) to 7 (big problem). **Bold** values and those with different superscripts differed significantly (p ≤ 0.05). n = 145-610.

Table 21. Evidence and severity of problems (mean; standard error); day and overnight users.

Problem	Percent who noticed		Mean problem severity	
	Day	Overnight	Day	Overnight
Trail wear and tear	78	79	**2.7**(.06)	**3.2**(.10)
Having to fill out permit/registration	74	75	1.8(.06)	1.9(.07)
Large numbers of day users	**69**	**63**	2.5(.06)	2.6(.10)
Trampled areas from camping/walking	69	68	**2.4**(.07)	**2.8**(.09)
Trails that are poorly marked	63	66	**2.3**(.07)	**2.7**(.11)
Large groups	**63**	**53**	**2.2**(.07)	**2.5**(.10)
Litter left behind by visitors	60	62	**2.1**(.07)	**2.6**(.11)
Uncontrolled dogs	61	60	2.1(.07)	2.1(.10)
Rules that restrict where people camp	57	54	**1.9**(.07)	**2.5**(.10)
Inconsiderate behavior by others	54	53	**2.0**(.08)	**2.4**(.11)
Too many rules and regulations	54	52	**1.8**(.07)	**2.1**(.10)
Contact with ranger or volunteer	54	52	**1.4**(.04)	**1.6**(.09)
Impacts from recreational packstock	**55**	**59**	**2.2**(.08)	**3.0**(.13)
Concern about your personal security	54	52	1.4(.05)	1.5(.07)
Noisy groups	**50**	**49**	**2.3**(.08)	**2.6**(.12)
Large numbers of overnight visitors	51	53	**1.7**(.07)	**2.4**(.10)
Human waste	50	49	**1.8**(.08)	**2.2**(.11)
Rules/regs not adequately enforced	49	48	**1.9**(.08)	**2.3**(.11)
Organized groups or outfitted parties	48	47	**1.6**(.06)	**1.8**(.10)

Scale for problem severity from 1 (not at all a problem) to 7 (big problem). **Bold** values differed significantly (p ≤ 0.05). n = 262-876

how **important it is** (on a 7-point scale from "not at all" to "extremely") and how often they **experience it** (on a 7-point scale from "never" to "always").

Most of these experiences were highly sought (table 22). The most highly sought experiences were "closeness to nature," "to be away from crowds of people," "a sense of being away from the modern world," and "a sense of freedom." The only experiences that were, on average, well below the mid-point of 4.0 were "to be near others who could help if I need them" and "to be my own boss." Most experiences were more highly sought by visitors to moderate use trailheads than by visitors to very high use trailheads. Similarly, three experiences were more highly sought by low use visitors than by all visitors (table 22). In particular, the motivations "to be away from crowds of people," to experience "solitude," and to have a "sense of remoteness" increased in importance as trailhead use level decreased. Apparently, some people selecting less popular locations were more interested in experiencing less crowded and impacted conditions. In contrast, experiences such as "a sense of challenge," "developing personal spiritual values," and "to think about who I am" did not differ much with use level.

When asked about the degree to which experiences were achieved, results were similar to those for experiences sought (table 23). Visitors to less heavily used trailheads generally had higher achievement scores, particularly for "to be away from crowds of people," "solitude," and "sense of remoteness." Readers should be cautioned about comparing results from the mailback questionnaire (where visitors were asked about wilderness trips in general) with those from the trailhead survey (where visitors were asked about their current trip).

We were also interested in the degree to which visitors actually had the experiences that were important to them. To explore this, we subtracted each person's score for experience sought from his/her score for experience achievement. A negative value suggests that visitors did not actually get the experience to the degree that they were seeking it, while a positive value indicates that desires were exceeded. Overall, the experiences that were least achieved, in relation to what were sought, were "to be away from crowds of people," "solitude," "sense of remoteness," and "a sense that the surroundings haven't been impacted by people" (table 24). These are all experiences that were more likely to be both sought and attained at less popular trailheads. Problems with attaining these experiences were most pronounced at very high use trailheads. Even for these experiences, however, the small values suggest that most visitors are having the experiences they were seeking.

For almost all experiences, day users' importance ratings were lower than overnight users' ratings (table 25). This suggests generally lower expectations regarding the experiences that might be attained on a day trip as opposed to an overnight trip. Day users also reported lower levels of experience achievement than overnight users. Because motivational differences were larger than differences in achievement, overnight

Table 22. Trip motivations (extent experiences were sought); use level variation.

Experience	Very high	High	Moderate	All visitors	Low use
Closeness to nature	**5.7**(.03)[a]	**6.0**(.03)[b]	**5.9**(.04)[ab]	6.2(.04)	6.3(.07)
Away from crowds	**5.1**(.04)[a]	**5.6**(.04)[b]	**5.9**(.04)[c]	**6.2**(.04)	**6.4**(.06)
Sense of being away from modern world	**5.2**(.03)[a]	**5.5**(.04)[b]	**5.6**(.04)[b]	5.9(.04)	6.1(.07)
Sense of freedom	**5.2**(.03)[a]	**5.3**(.03)[b]	**5.4**(.04)[b]	5.6(.03)	5.8(.07)
Wilderness opportunities	**4.8**(.04)[a]	**5.1**(.04)[b]	**5.2**(.05)[b]	5.4(.05)	5.5(.09)
Sense of remoteness	**4.7**(.04)[a]	**5.1**(.04)[b]	**5.3**(.04)[c]	5.7(.05)	**5.9**(.08)
Solitude	**4.6**(.03)[a]	**5.0**(.04)[b]	**5.3**(.05)[c]	5.7(.04)	**6.0**(.07)
Sense of challenge	**5.0**(.04)[a]	**4.8**(.04)[b]	**4.8**(.05)[b]	5.1(.05)	5.2(.09)
Sense of surroundings not impacted by people	**4.6**(.04)[a]	**5.1**(.04)[b]	**5.1**(.05)[b]	5.8(.05)	5.8(.09)
Learn about this place	**4.2**(.04)[a]	**4.5**(.05)[b]	**4.5**(.05)[b]	5.1(.05)	5.3(.08)
Develop personal spiritual values	3.6(.04)	3.8(.05)	3.7(.06)	4.6(.07)	4.6(.13)
Think about who I am	3.4(.04)	3.4(.05)	3.4(.05)	4.2(.06)	4.1(.12)
Be my own boss	3.0(.04)	3.1(.05)	3.1(.06)	3.8(.07)	4.0(.13)
Be near others who could help if needed	2.6(.03)	2.6(.04)	2.5(.05)	2.7(.05)	2.6(.10)

Values are mean (standard error) rating from 1 (not at all) to 7 (very much) for "how much were you seeking" each experience?
Bold values and those with different superscripts are significantly different (p ≤ 0.05). n = 237-1580.

Table 23. Experience achievement; use level variation.

Experience	Very high	High	Moderate	All visitors	Low use
Closeness to nature	5.7(.03)a	6.0(.03)b	5.9(.04)b	5.2(.03)	5.2(.06)
Away from crowds	4.5(.04)a	5.0(.04)b	5.5(.04)c	**4.4(.05)**	**4.6(.09)**
Sense of being away from modern world	5.2(.03)a	5.5(.04)b	5.5(.04)b	4.7(.04)	4.8(.07)
Sense of freedom	5.2(.03)a	5.5(.03)b	5.5(.04)b	4.7(.03)	4.7(.07)
Wilderness opportunities	4.8(.03)a	5.1(.04)b	5.3(.04)c	4.4(.04)	4.5(.07)
Sense of remoteness	4.5(.03)a	4.8(.04)b	5.1(.04)c	**4.3(.04)**	**4.5(.07)**
Solitude	4.3(.03)a	4.6(.04)b	5.1(.04)c	**4.3(.04)**	**4.5(.07)**
Sense of challenge	5.0(.04)a	4.9(.04)b	4.8(.05)b	4.4(.04)	4.5(.07)
Sense of surroundings not impacted by people	4.2(.04)a	4.6(.04)b	4.6(.05)b	3.8(.04)	4.0(.08)
Learn about this place	4.4(.04)a	4.7(.04)b	4.7(.05)b	4.6(.04)	4.6(.07)
Develop personal spiritual values	3.7(.04)	4.0(.05)	3.8(.06)	4.1(.05)	4.1(.10)
Think about who I am	3.6(0.4)	3.7(.05)	3.7(.06)	3.9(.05)	3.8(.10)
Be my own boss	3.4(.04)	3.4(.04)	3.4(.05)	4.0(.04)	4.0(.09)
Be near others who could help if needed	3.1(.04)a	3.2(.05)ab	2.9(.05)b	3.1(.05)	3.0(.10)

Values are mean (standard error) rating from 1 (not at all) to 7 (very much) for "how much did you experience it?" **Bold** values and those with different superscripts are significantly different (p ≤ 0.05). n = 233-2454.

Table 24. Extent to which experiences sought were achieved; use level variation.

Experience	Very high	High	Moderate	All visitors	Low use
Closeness to nature	-.05(.02)	-.06(.02)	-.03(.02)	-1.00(.03)	-1.06(.06)
Away from crowds	**-.55(.03)a**	**-.66(.04)a**	**-.39(.04)b**	-1.74(.05)	-1.78(.08)
Sense of being away from modern world	-.09(.02)	-.10(.03)	-.05(.03)	-1.21(.05)	-1.24(.07)
Sense of freedom	.04(.02)	.10(.02)	.07(.03)	-0.88(.05)	-1.02(.08)
Wilderness opportunities	.02(.02)	-.03(.02)	.02(.02)	-0.99(.04)	-1.00(.07)
Sense of remoteness	**-.28(.03)ab**	**-.34(.03)a**	**-.20(.04)b**	-1.36(.05)	-1.44(.08)
Solitude	**-.42(.03)a**	**-.43(.03)a**	**-.24(.04)b**	-1.45(.05)	-1.54(.08)
Sense of challenge	-.02(.02)	.07(.03)	.07(.03)	-0.72(.04)	-0.76(.07)
Sense of surroundings not impacted by people	**-.36(.03)a**	**-.51(.04)b**	**-.47(.04)b**	-2.00(.06)	-1.84(.08)
Learn about this place	.23(.02)	.16(.02)	.19(.03)	**-0.57(.04)**	**-0.74(.07)**
Develop personal spiritual values	.10(.02)	.08(.02)	.11(.03)	-0.55(.04)	-0.56(.06)
Think about who I am	.23(.02)	.24(.03)	.26(.03)	-0.33(.04)	-0.35(.07)
Be my own boss	.29(.02)	.28(.03)	.32(.03)	0.08(.06)	-0.08(.10)
Be near others who could help if needed	.57(.03)	.57(.04)	.48(.04)	0.37(.05)	0.45(.10)

Values are the experience achievement score minus the experience sought score, both on 7-point scales. Negative values indicate hoped for experiences were not obtained. **Bold** values and those with different superscripts are significantly different (p ≤ 0.05). n = 233-2437.

users had more substantial problems than did day users with having the experiences that they desired.

Solitude

We were particularly interested in the importance of solitude to visitors—the degree to which they expected and experienced it. When asked to select one of four responses on this issue, about one-half of respondents reported that "solitude was important to me on this visit, and I found it" (table 26). Most remaining respondents reported that solitude was not important to them or that they did not expect it. Only 5 percent of respondents chose "solitude was important to me but I did not find it." The proportion seeking but not finding solitude was small regardless of use level or length of stay. However, day users and visitors to more popular places were much more likely to state that solitude was not important to them on this visit. Conversely, overnight users and visitors to moderate use trailheads were most likely to state that solitude was important to them and that they found it. The

Table 25. Differences between day and overnight users in extent to which various experiences were sought and achieved.

Experience	Sought		Achieved		Difference	
	Day	Overnight	Day	Overnight	Day	Overnight
Closeness to nature	5.8(.02)	5.9(.03)	5.8(.02)	5.9(.03)	-.04(.02)	-.06(.02)
Away from crowds	**5.3**(0.3)	**5.7**(.04)	**4.8**(.03)	**5.0**(.04)	**-.46**(.03)	**-.70**(.04)
Sense of being away from modern world	**5.3**(.03)	**5.7**(.04)	**5.2**(.03)	**5.6**(.03)	-.07(.02)	-.11(.03)
Sense of freedom	**5.2**(.03)	**5.4**(.04)	**5.3**(.02)	**5.5**(.03)	.09(.02)	.01(.03)
Wilderness opportunities	**4.8**(.03)	**5.3**(.04)	**4.9**(.03)	**5.3**(.04)	**.03**(.02)	**-.03**(.02)
Sense of remoteness	**4.8**(.03)	**5.4**(.04)	**4.6**(.03)	**5.0**(.04)	**-.21**(.02)	**-.42**(.04)
Solitude	**4.8**(.03)	**5.2**(.04)	**4.5**(.03)	**4.7**(.04)	**-.34**(.03)	**-.47**(.04)
Sense of challenge	4.7(.03)	**5.4**(.04)	4.7(.03)	**5.4**(.04)	**.00**(.02)	**.08**(.03)
Sense of surroundings not impacted by people	**4.7**(.03)	**5.1**(.04)	**4.4**(.03)	**4.5**(.04)	**-.32**(.03)	**-.65**(.04)
Learn about this place	**4.3**(.03)	**4.5**(.04)	**4.5**(.03)	**4.8**(.04)	**.17**(.02)	**.35**(.03)
Develop personal spiritual values	**3.6**(.03)	**3.9**(.05)	3.7(.03)	3.8(.05)	.10(.02)	.07(.02)
Think about who I am	**3.3**(.03)	**3.5**(.05)	**3.6**(.03)	**3.8**(.05)	**.22**(.02)	**.29**(.03)
Be my own boss	**3.0**(.03)	**3.3**(.04)	**3.3**(.03)	**3.6**(.05)	.29(.02)	.30(.02)
Be near others who could help if needed	2.5(.03)	2.6(.05)	3.0(.03)	3.2(.05)	.52(.02)	.60(.03)

Values are the experience achievement score minus the experience sought score, both on 7-point scales. Negative values indicate hoped for experiences that were not obtained. **Bold** values are significantly different (p ≤ 0.05). n = 1712-3621.

Table 26. Solitude importance, expectations, and whether or not it was experienced.

Percent selecting the following regarding the importance of solitude on this visit	Very high	High	Moderate	Day	Overnight
A sense of solitude was not important to me on this visit	32	27	17	32	17
I hoped to find solitude, but did not expect it on this visit	23	17	18	20	20
Solitude was important to me on this visit, and I found it	40	50	62	44	56
Solitude was important to me on this visit but I did not find it	5	6	3	4	6

Responses varied significantly among use levels and between day and overnight users (p ≤ 0.05). n = 603-1870.

difference among use levels for this question was one of the larger observed differences for any question in the study.

We also explored, using a general, more hypothetical question, the importance of solitude to having a wilderness experience, as well as the conditions that were conducive to having a profound sense of solitude. For this purpose, visitors were shown five different statements. For each, they were asked the extent to which they agreed or disagreed with the statement, recorded on a 7-point scale from +3 (strongly agree) to -3 (strongly disagree). Only one-half of respondents agreed with the statement, "I cannot have a real wilderness experience unless I have a profound sense of solitude." While one might have expected more agreement with this statement, it is worth noting that few respondents strongly disagreed with this statement. Moreover, more respondents might have agreed with this statement if we had not used the word "profound" to describe the sense of solitude that is important to the wilderness experience. It is also worth noting that respondents were allowed to define a real wilderness experience any way they wanted. Their definition might differ substantially from that of the reader or the framers of the Wilderness Act. The statement most often supported was "solitude adds to the wilderness experience, but is not critical."

Regarding statements about conditions that are conducive to solitude, opinions were more widely divergent. Equal numbers agreed and disagreed with the statement, "I can have a profound sense of solitude in wilderness, even if there are many other groups of people around." When stated inversely and more stringently as "I cannot have a profound sense of solitude unless there are no other groups around," the majority disagreed. The strongest consensus was disagreement with the statement, "I cannot have a profound sense of solitude unless I am completely alone." Our intent with this question was to differentiate between being completely alone (away even from members of your own group) and being with your group but away from other groups.

Low use visitors did not differ significantly from all visitors in their agreement with any of these statements about solitude (table 27). Very high use visitors were significantly more likely than visitors to less popular trails to agree that solitude is not critical to the wilderness experience and that they can have profound solitude, even with many other groups around. They were also significantly less likely to agree that they cannot have a real wilderness experience.

Day and overnight visitors differed significantly in agreement with these statements about solitude (table 28). Day users were more likely to agree that solitude was not critical to having a real wilderness experience, more likely to agree that they can find solitude even if there are lots of other people around, and less likely to agree that they cannot have a real wilderness experience without having a profound sense of solitude (table 28). As was the case with use levels, even the statistically significant differences were small.

Encounters with Other Groups

Given our interest in understanding how use density influences the experiences people have in wilderness, we asked a number of questions about encounters with other groups—how many occurred and their effect. As expected, encounter levels increased as trailhead use increased (fig. 1). To interpret figure 1, note that encounter levels refer to the number of groups rather than the number of people. The question asked about encounters on the day of the exit survey, not encounters over the entire trip. Since the mean group size of

Table 27. Agreement with statements about solitude (mean, standard error); use level variation.

	Very high	High	Moderate	All visitors	Low use
I cannot have a real wilderness experience unless I have a profound sense of solitude	**0.3**(.06)[a]	**0.5**(.08)[ab]	**0.6**(.09)[b]	0.4(.06)	0.6(.10)
Solitude adds to the wilderness experience, but is not critical	**1.2**(.06)[a]	**1.0**(.08)[ab]	**1.0**(.10)[b]	0.8(.06)	0.9(.11)
I can have a profound sense of solitude in wilderness, even if there are many other groups of people around	**0.2**(.07)[a]	**-0.0**(.09)[b]	**-0.1**(.10)[b]	-1.0(.06)	-0.9(.10)
I cannot have a profound sense of solitude unless there are no other groups of people around	-0.5(.06)	-0.3(.08)	-0.3(.09)	0.0(.06)	-0.0(.11)
I cannot have a profound sense of solitude unless I am completely alone)	-1.0(.07)	-1.0(.08)	-1.0(.10)	-0.7(.06)	-0.8(.11

7-point scale from -3 (strongly disagree) to +3 (strongly agree). **Bold** values with different superscripts are significantly different ($p \leq 0.05$). n = 234-804.

Table 28. Agreement with statements about solitude (mean, standard error); day and overnight users.

	Day	Overnight
I cannot have a real wilderness experience unless I have a profound sense of solitude	**0.4**(.05)	**0.6**(.08)[b]
Solitude adds to the wilderness experience, but is not critical	**1.2**(.05)	**0.9**(.09)
I can have a profound sense of solitude in wilderness, even if there are many other groups of people around	**0.2**(.05)	**-0.2**(.09)
I cannot have a profound sense of solitude unless there are no other groups of people around	**-0.5**(.05)	**-0.2**(.08)
I cannot have a profound sense of solitude unless I am completely alone	-1.0(.05)	-1.0(.09)

7-point scale from -3 (strongly disagree) to +3 (strongly agree). **Bold** values are significantly different ($p \leq 0.05$). n = 360-915.

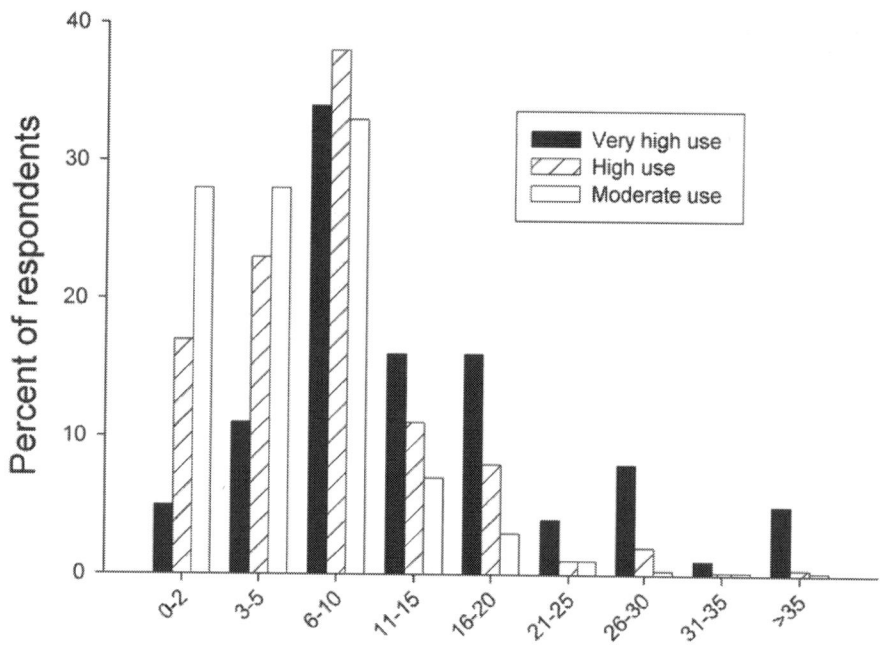

Figure 1. Number of other groups encountered per day; use level variation.

our sample was 3.4, these values can be multiplied by 3.4 to approximate the number of people that were encountered per day. The encounter scale had a maximum value of "more than 40," a response for which we assigned a value of 45. It is also worth remembering that these are the number of encounters respondents thought they had, a number that is often quite different from the number of encounters they actually had (Cole and others 1997).

Figure 2 is a cumulative frequency distribution for the data presented in figure 1. This graph can be used to assess the proportion of respondents who had more or less than any particular number of encounters per day. For example, reading up from a value of 10 encounters on the X axis, only 11 percent of respondents at moderate use trailheads encountered 10 or more groups per day, while about 50 percent of respondents at very high use trailheads encountered at least 10 groups per day. Reading across from 50 percent of respondents on the Y axis, one-half of respondents at moderate use trailheads encountered at least four groups, while one-half of the respondents at very high use trailheads encountered at least 10 groups. High use trailheads differed from very high use trailheads

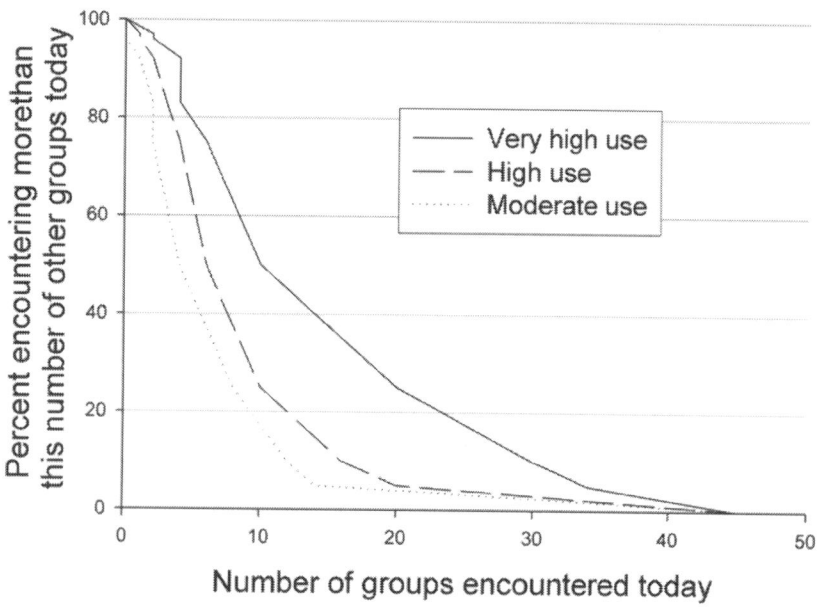

Figure 2. Cumulative frequency distribution of number of other groups encountered per day; use level variation.

Table 29. Encounters with other groups (mean, standard error).

	Very high	High	Moderate	Day	Overnight
Percent of time in sight of groups today	**30**(.8)[a]	**18**(.8)[b]	**12**(.8)[c]	21(.6)	24(1.0)
Number of groups seen today	**14**(.3)[a]	**8**(.2)[b]	**6**(.2)[c]	11(.2)	10(.3)
Number of groups seen on a typical day	**12**(.6)[a]	**8**(.4)[b]	**5**(.3)[c]	-	9(0.3)
Fewest groups seen in a day	**8**(.5)[a]	**5**(.3)[b]	**4**(.3)[c]	-	6(0.2)
Number of other groups camped in sight or sound last night	**2.4**(.2)[a]	**1.8**(.2)[b]	**1.3**(.1)[b]	-	1.9(0.1)

Values with different superscripts are significantly different (p ≤ 0.05). n = 617-1902.

more than they differed from moderate use trailheads. Encountering no other groups was a rare occurrence, even at the moderate use trailheads.

The median number of other groups encountered per day was four at moderate use trailheads, compared to six at high use trailheads and 10 at very high use trailheads. Means were slightly higher (table 29). We also asked people about the proportion of time that other groups were in sight and sound. As with estimates of number of groups seen, these varied significantly with use level. Encounter levels did not vary much between day and overnight users (table 29).

For overnight users, we asked about the number seen on a "typical" day and the fewest groups seen on any day. Our thinking was that overnight visitors would see more people on the last day of their trip as they passed through portal areas, but they might have spent time in low use interior areas during at least part of their trip. Thus, they might have had more opportunities for solitude at those times. The typical number seen differed slightly from "the number seen today," which is not surprising given that most people were out for just a night or two. But the fewest seen on at least one day of the trip was substantially lower.

Finally, we asked about the number of other groups camped within sight and sound on the previous night (the last night of the trip). The number of campsite encounters varied significantly with trailhead use level (table 29). Camping alone was more common for visitors to moderate use trailheads and camping with more than five other groups was more common for very high use trailheads (fig. 3). However, regardless of trailhead use level, most groups camped within sight and sound of at least one other group.

Effects of Encounters

We asked visitors how the number of groups they saw on their trip affected their enjoyment, sense that they were in wilderness, and sense of solitude and freedom—important attributes of wilderness. Enjoyment

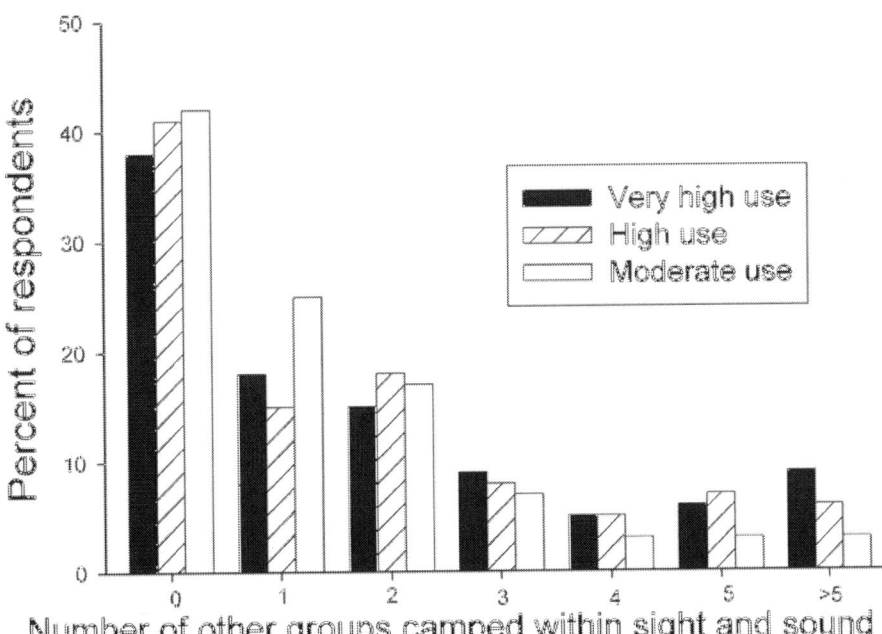

Figure 3. Number of other groups camped within sight or sound; use level variation.

Table 30. Effects of the number of other groups seen.

Effect of the number of people seen on:	Very high	High	Moderate	Day	Overnight
My enjoyment	0.2(.04)	0.1(.05)	0.2(.06)	0.2(.03)	0.1(.06)
My sense that I was in Wilderness	**-0.3**(.05)[a]	**-0.3**(.06)[a]	**-0.1**(.07)[b]	**-0.1**(.04)	**-0.3**(.06)
My sense of solitude	-0.4(.05)	-0.3(.07)	-0.3(.07)	**-0.2**(.04)	**-0.5**(.07)
My sense of freedom	-0.1(.04)	-0.1(.05)	0.0(.05)	-0.0(.03)	-0.1(.05)

Values are mean (standard error) rating from +3 (added a lot) to -3 (detracted a lot). **Bold** values and those with different superscripts are significantly significant ($p \leq 0.05$). n = 295-889.

was slightly affected by the number of groups seen (table 30). The number of people reporting that the number of groups they saw added to their enjoyment exceeded the number reporting that it detracted. When the question addressed effect on wilderness solitude and freedom, more visitors reported that the number of people they saw detracted. However, the most common response was always the neutral response and very few people reported a high degree of detraction. Differences in the effect of the number of groups seen, among use levels and length of stay, were either not statistically significant or small (table 30).

Multiple regression analyses confirmed the adverse effects of increased encounter levels on visitor experiences. We found statistically significant negative linear relationships between both the number of groups encountered and the percent of time other groups were in sight and evaluations of effects of the number of groups seen on enjoyment and sense of being in wilderness with respect to solitude and freedom (table 31). However, coefficients of determination (R^2) were very small. Encounter levels did not explain more than 3 percent of the variance for any of the relationships. In part, this is because so many people simply said that encounters had no overall effect on them.

Regression coefficients were also very small. To illustrate this graphically, we divided the number of groups encountered into 10 categories, each with roughly equivalent numbers of observations. For each use category (such as seven to nine groups encountered), we calculated means and standard deviations. These were plotted on graphs using the midpoint of each use category and fitted with straight lines. In effect, this separated the variability associated with differences between respondents (illustrated by the standard deviations) from the effect of use on experience (how well the mean values can be fitted to a model—in our case, a straight line). The magnitude of effect was greatest for the sense of being in wilderness. Figure 4 shows that one's sense of being in wilderness tends to decline with increasing encounters, but not by much. Regression equations predict that it would take an increase in number of encounters of 50 groups per day to cause just a 1.0 unit decrease on the 7-point scale.

To focus more narrowly on the magnitude of crowding-related problems, we asked visitors to assess the extent to which they were adversely affected by other groups that they encountered on their trip. This question was worded such that the adverse effect

Table 31. Multiple regression results relating use level to the effect of number of groups seen on experience[a].

	Groups encountered per day		Time in sight of other groups	
Effect of encounters on:	ΔR^2	β	ΔR^2	β
Sense of enjoyment	0.007	-0.08	-	-
Sense that I was in wilderness	0.024	-0.12	0.004	-0.07
Sense of solitude	0.017	-0.09	0.005	-0.08
Sense of freedom	0.009	-0.10	-	-

[a] Values are (1) the change in R^2 (variance explained) that results from adding significant variables to the stepwise model and (2) standardized beta coefficients of the full model (illustrating directionality and magnitude of effect). Negative beta indicates that encounters detracted more from experiences as use increased. n = 2641-2656.

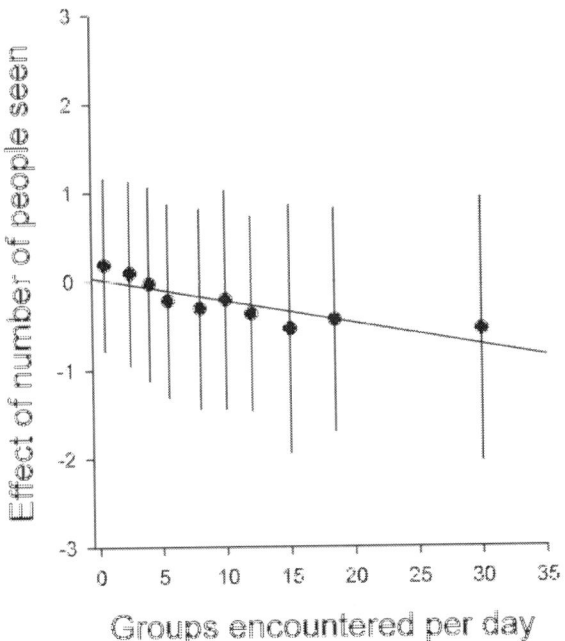

Figure 4. Effect of number of encounters on "sense that I was in Wilderness"—from +3 (encounters added a lot) to -3 (encounters detracted a lot).

Multiple regression analyses showed that the adverse effects of other groups increased with increases in the number of groups encountered and percent of time other groups were in sight (table 33). For these more specific behavioral responses, effects of encounters were somewhat greater than effects on enjoyment, solitude, freedom, and the sense of being in wilderness (table 31). However, even for the experience most sensitive to encounter levels—the ability to be free from disruptions and distractions–encounter levels explained only 10 percent of the variance. The magnitude of effect was also small. For freedom from disruptions and distraction, regression equations predict that an increase in number of encounters of 25 groups per day would cause only a 1.0 unit increase in the 7-unit scale (fig. 5).

Encounter Preferences and Evaluative Standards

Given the interest in and difficulty of developing encounter standards, we asked visitors questions related to their preferences and response to various levels of encounters with other groups. Specifically, we asked questions regarding:

- the encounter level they **prefer** in wilderness
- the encounter level that **begins to detract** from their experience
- the encounter level that **would displace** them—cause them to not come if they knew it would occur

Respondents were given the option of reporting that "the number of other groups I see doesn't matter to me."

Visitors contacted at very high use trailheads were more likely to state that the number of groups they see doesn't matter to them compared to visitors to less popular trailheads (table 34). Exiting visitors were much more likely to report that encounters do not matter than

could result from the behavior of a particular group, as well as the number of groups. For all items (table 32), the majority of respondents reported no adverse effect at all. Effects on the "ability to sit and be quiet, free from disruptions and distractions" were most substantial. However, no more than 10 to 15 percent reported even moderately adverse effects. Some adverse effects were significantly higher for visitors to very high use trailheads and for overnight users (table 32), but differences were small. In two-factor analyses of variance, use level effects interacted with length of stay effects. More detailed analysis showed that day users were less adversely affected than overnight users in moderate use places. In very high use places, however, day users were more adversely affected.

Table 32. Magnitude of adverse effects of the number of other groups seen.

Adverse effect of the number of people seen on:	Very high	High	Moderate	Day	Overnight
Ability to set own pace	**0.8**(.04)[a]	**0.6**(.04)[b]	**0.5**(.04)[b]	0.7(.03)	0.6(.04)
Ability to choose where to do the things you want to do (camp, picnic, fish, swim, etc.)	0.8(.04)	0.9(.05)	0.9(.07)	**0.8**(.03)	**1.3**(.06)
Ability to sit and be quiet	**1.1**(.04)[a]	**1.0**(.06)[ab]	**0.9**(.06)[b]	1.0(04)	1.2(.06)
Freedom from disruptions and distractions	**1.3**(.05)[a]	**1.2**(.06)[ab]	**1.0**(.06)[b]	1.1(.04)	**1.4**(.06)
Freedom to behave as you wanted	1.0(.04)	0.9(.05)	0.8(.06)	**0.8**(.03)	**1.1**(.06)
Freedom to decide with whom to interact	0.8(.04)	0.7(.05)	0.6(.05)	0.7(.03)	0.8(.05)

Values are mean (standard error) rating from 0 (no effect) to 6 (great adverse effect). **Bold** values and those with different superscripts are significantly different ($p \leq 0.05$). n = 592-1836.

Table 33. Multiple regression results relating use level to the adverse effect of number of groups encountered on specific aspects of the experience[a].

Effect of encounters on:	Groups encountered per day		Time in sight of other groups	
	ΔR²	β	ΔR²	β
Ability to set your own pace along the trail	0.055	0.16	0.016	0.15
Choice of where to do the things you wanted to do	0.006	0.10	0.046	0.16
Ability to sit and be quiet	0.010	0.12	0.082	0.23
Freedom from disruptions/distractions	0.011	0.12	0.086	0.23
Freedom to behave as you wanted	0.005	0.08	0.047	0.17
Freedom to decide with whom to interact	0.006	0.09	0.042	0.16

[a] Values are (1) the change in R² (variance explained) that results from adding significant variables to the stepwise model and (2) standardized beta coefficients of the full model (illustrating directionality and magnitude of effect). Positive beta indicates that the adverse effects of encounters increased as use increased. n = 2621-2660.

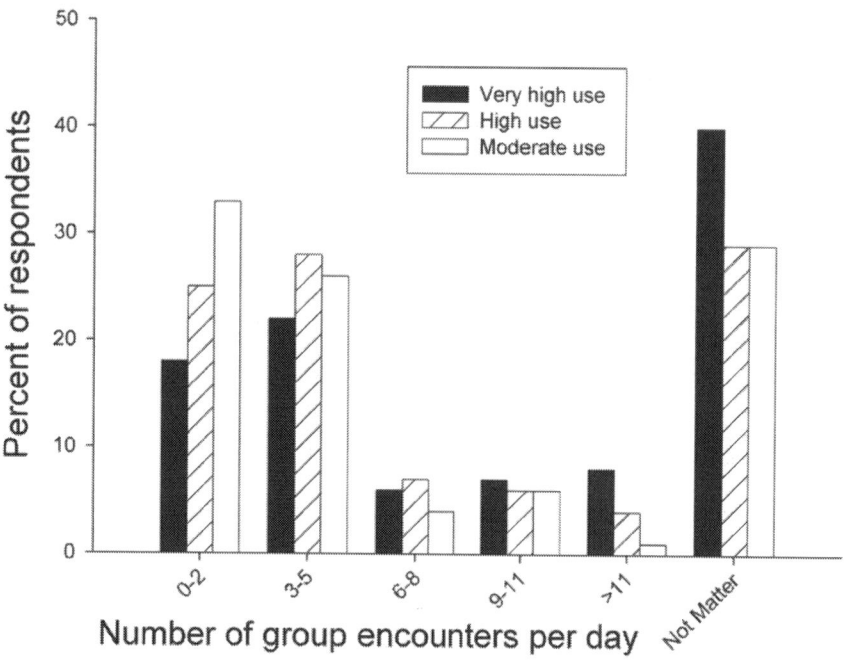

Figure 5. Magnitude of adverse effect of number of groups encountered on "freedom from disruptions or distractions"—from 0 (not at all) to 6 (greatly).

people completing the mailback questionnaire. This may reflect the difference between a trailhead survey (administered immediately after the trip) and a mailback survey (administered up to a year after the trip) and/or the difference between group leaders and group members. Another possibility is that it reflects the time lag between one's trip and one's evaluation. Visitors to low use trailheads were as likely as the entire population of wilderness visitors to report that encounters don't matter. Day and overnight users were equally likely to report that encounters don't matter (table 35).

As expected, encounter preferences were lower than estimates of the number of encounters that would begin to detract from the experience, which were lower than estimates of the number of encounters that would cause visitors to be displaced (they would choose not to visit if they knew they would see that many) (table 36). For each of these evaluations, standards increased significantly (more encounters were more acceptable) as use level increased (table 36). It is also clear that respondents to the exit survey were more tolerant of more encounters compared to respondents to the mailback survey. Again, this might reflect less tolerance among group leaders, more tolerance immediately after the experience or both.

Most use level differences were small. Regardless of trailhead use level, either most visitors did not care how many other people they saw or they wanted to see

Table 34. Percent of visitors for whom number of encounters does not matter; use level variation.

	Very high	High	Moderate	All visitors	Low use
Percent of visitors	**40**[a]	**29**[b]	**29**[b]	16	14

Bold values and those with different superscripts are significantly different ($p \leq 0.05$).
n = 111-1298.

Table 35. Percent of visitors for whom number of encounters does not matter; day and overnight users.

	Day	Overnight
Percent of visitors	35	32

Percentages are not significantly different ($p \leq 0.05$).
n = 840-1874.

Table 36. Median numerical standards for groups encountered per day; use level variation.

Evaluative dimension	Very high	High	Moderate	All visitors	Low use
Preference	**4**[a]	**3**[b]	**3**[c]	3	2
Begins to detract	**10**[a]	**10**[b]	**10**[c]	6	4
Would displace	**20**[a]	**15**[b]	**10**[c]	10	9

Visitors reporting that number of encounters does not matter are excluded. Refer to text for the evaluative dimensions.
Bold values and those with different superscripts are significantly different (Kruskal-Wallis, $p \leq 0.05$). n = 92-435.

very few other people (fig. 6). This bimodal distribution of responses illustrates the difficulty of interpreting these data. Whom should we manage for—the large minority who don't care how many encounters they have or the large minority who want to have very few encounters? If we split the difference and manage for the median user—say 15 to 25 encounters per day—we will be providing experiences that are preferred by very few people. As figure 7 suggests, for the number of encounters that begin to detract from the experience, variation among individual respondents dwarfs variation related to use level.

Differences between day and overnight users were also statistically significant but small (table 37). Day users, on average, were more tolerant of higher levels of encounters than overnight users.

Displacement

We asked visitors about several types and spatial scales of displacement. We asked about within-wilderness spatial displacement—"have you intentionally avoided trails or areas in this wilderness for any reason?" If they had been displaced, we asked them to state where they had been displaced from and why. We asked about within-wilderness temporal displacement—"have you ever changed the timing of your visits to this wilderness to avoid times of heavy use?" We asked them about spatial and temporal displacement in other wilderness areas—"are there other wilderness areas that have places or times that you avoid because of the amount of use?" If so, we asked which wildernesses were avoided. Finally, we investigated displacement from entire wilderness areas by asking "have you ever decided not to visit this wilderness because of the amount of use?" For the question about displacement from other wildernesses, we used all respondents' answers. However, for the questions regarding displacement from or within the wilderness where we contacted them, we only report results for repeat users—respondents who had visited the area at least three times before.

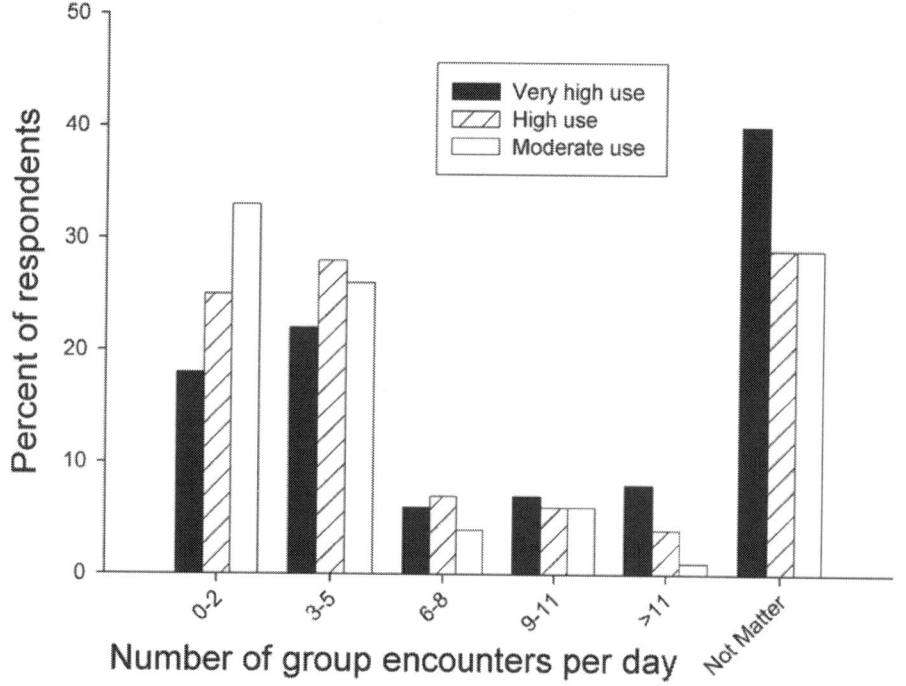

Figure 6. Preference for number of groups encountered per day; use level variation.

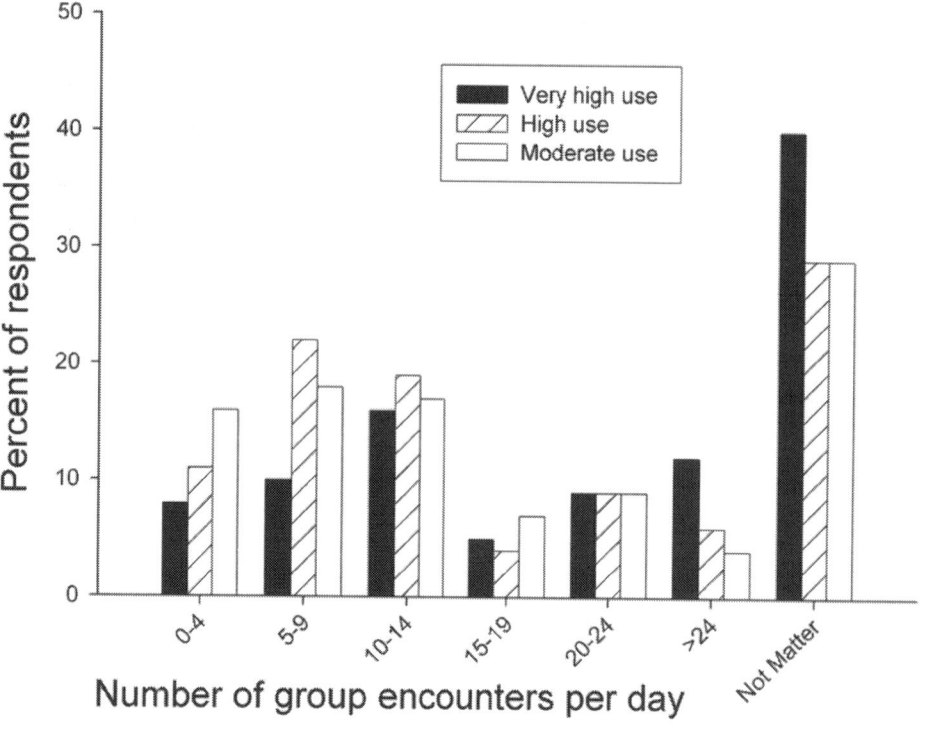

Figure 7. Maximum number of groups encountered per day that would begin to detract from the experience; use level variation.

Table 37. Median numerical standards for groups encountered per day; day and overnight users.

	Day	Overnight
Preference	4	3
Begins to detract	10	10
Would displace	**20**	**15**

Visitors reporting that number of encounters does not matter are excluded. Refer to text for the evaluative dimensions.
Bold values are significantly different (Mann-Whitney, $p \leq 0.05$). n = 325-667.

For repeat visitors, about 27 percent reported within-wilderness spatial displacement (table 38). Of those who avoided places in this wilderness, 58 percent gave crowding as a reason. The only other reasons for displacement reported by more than a few people were terrain, snow, impacts, stock, water, and regulations on dogs. Each of these was reported by 3- to 4 percent of those reporting displacement. Spatial displacement was more common in the more heavily used places (table 38). Moreover, the proportion of displaced visitors reporting crowding as the reason for displacement increased with use level: 64 percent (very high), 53 percent (high), and 48 percent (moderate). Overnight users were more likely to be spatially displaced than day users but they were less likely to report that crowding was the reason for displacement: 52 percent (overnight users) and 61 percent (day users).

Adjusting the timing of use (for example, not visiting on weekends or holidays) was much more common than avoiding particular trails. Fifty-eight percent of those who had been to the trailhead where we contacted them at least three times before reported temporal displacement. Avoiding certain times was more common at the more popular trailheads and among day users (table 38). Twenty percent of first-time visitors reported avoiding times of heavy use, regardless of trailhead use level. This suggests that a substantial portion of the population (20 percent) has learned to avoid times of high use even at places they have never visited before and they employ this strategy regardless of use level. Repeat users relied on this strategy more, particularly at more popular trailheads.

A substantial minority of visitors (39 percent) reported avoiding crowded places and certain times in other wilderness areas (table 38). The most commonly mentioned wildernesses that were avoided were Mount Hood, Mount Rainier, Alpine Lakes, Mount Jefferson, and Three Sisters. Each was listed by 7 to 10 percent of the visitors who reported displacement, or about 1 percent of all visitors. A common assertion is that very high use trailheads are primarily used by people tolerant of crowds, with less tolerant users displaced to less popular locations. If this assertion were true, we would expect the proportion of users reporting displacement from crowded wilderness areas to be much higher at moderate use trailheads than at very high use trailheads. Displacement reported by visitors to moderate use trails was not significantly higher than that reported by visitors to more popular trails (table 38), so this assertion is not supported by our findings.

About 25 percent of repeat users reported that they had decided at some point in the past *not* to visit the wilderness where we contacted them due to the amount of use by other visitors. This type of displacement was more pronounced at the very high use trailheads (table 38). Collectively, these results suggest that users to these trailheads adjust where and when they visit wilderness when they feel the need to avoid heavy use, but few have been absolutely displaced to the degree that they no longer return. If substantial displacement had occurred, there would be fewer people reporting displacement among repeat users at the high use

Table 38. Visitor displacement (percent reporting).

Percent responding yes to the following:	Very high	High	Moderate	Day	Overnight
Have you ever avoided other wildernesses due to amount of use?	38	37	42	37	42
Have you ever avoided trails/places in this wilderness for any reason?[*]	**30**[a]	**25**[ab]	**22**[b]	**25**	**32**
Have you ever changed the time of visit to this wilderness due to amount of use?[*]	59[a]	66[a]	41[b]	59	53
Have you ever decided not to visit this wilderness due to amount of use?[*]	31[a]	19[b]	21[b]	25	25

Bold values and those with different superscripts are significantly different ($p \leq 0.05$). n = 632-1782.
*Percent of those who had been to this destination or area at least 3 times before.

trailheads and more users of moderate use trailheads reporting that there were other wilderness areas they avoided.

Attitudes Toward Management of Recreation in Wilderness

We were interested in visitor opinions about the acceptability of nine specific management actions. We asked the questions in the context of "this wilderness" (in other words, the wilderness the person had just visited), but did not specify why these actions might be taken other than "to protect the wilderness." Not surprisingly, most visitors supported actions that were not restrictive or that restricted few activities or users (table 39). The only actions supported by a majority were installing information on bulletin boards within the wilderness, posting directional signs, prohibiting campfires, and confining camping to designated sites. No actions were opposed by a majority. The actions that were most opposed were prohibitions on dogs and limits on the number of day users. While limits on overnight use were more often supported than opposed, limits on day use were more often opposed than supported.

Support for three of the nine management actions differed significantly with use level and length of stay (table 39). Support for constructing toilets, prohibiting campfires, and packing out human waste increased as trailhead use level increased and was greater among day users than overnight users. Support for the following three actions differed significantly with length of stay but not with use level. Day users were more likely than overnight users to support limiting overnight users, posting directional trail signs, and requiring the use of designated campsites. Differences were generally small, however.

Support for Zoning

To assess support for within-wilderness zoning, respondents were told "Forest Service managers must find an appropriate balance between allowing all people to visit the wilderness when they want and providing opportunities for solitude." They were then asked for their opinion about "which of the following options strikes the best balance for this wilderness?"

A. Do not restrict use to manage for solitude anywhere, even if use is heavy.
B. Manage for solitude along a few wilderness trails. The number of people allowed to use these few trails will be limited, but the majority of trails will have no use limits and may be heavily used.
C. Manage for solitude on most wilderness trails, by limiting the number of people using these trails. A few trails will have unrestricted use. Use levels will be high on these trails.
D. Manage for solitude everywhere in wilderness, even though this may mean that use will be restricted and people will be turned away."

The vast majority of visitors supported zoning and selected options that involve managing for variable conditions within the wilderness (table 40). Support was highest for managing a few trails for solitude. Support for not restricting use anywhere was higher than support for managing for solitude everywhere. Support for these options did not vary significantly with amount of use, but the people surveyed as they exited the wilderness were more supportive of manag-

Table 39. Support for management actions.

	Very high	High	Moderate	Day	Overnight
Install information about proper behavior on bulletin boards in wilderness	1.5(.06)	1.3(.08)	1.2(.10)	1.4(.05)	1.2(.09)
Post directional trail signs	1.3(.06)	1.3(.08)	1.3(.10)	**1.4**(.05)	**1.0**(.08)
Prohibit campfires	**0.9**(.07)[a]	**0.7**(.09)[a]	**0.3**(.11)[b]	**0.8**(.06)	**0.5**(.10)
Require camping in designated sites	0.8(.07)	0.5(.10)	0.4(.12)	**0.9**(.06)	**-0.1**(.10)
Require people to pack out their human waste	**0.7**(.08)[a]	**0.4**(.10)[b]	**0.0**(.12)[b]	**0.7**(.07)	**-0.2**(.10)
Limit the number of overnight users	0.1(.07)	-0.1(.09)	0.0(.10)	**0.1**(.06)	**-0.2**(.09)
Construct toilets in the wilderness	**0.0**(.07)[a]	**-0.3**(.10)[b]	**-0.3**(.10)[ab]	-0.1(.06)	-0.4(.10)
Prohibit dogs	-0.2(.08)	-0.4(.10)	-0.4(.12)	-0.3(.07)	-0.3(.10)
Limit the number of day users	-0.4(.07)	-0.5(.08)	-0.4(.10)	-0.5(.06)	-0.3(.09)

Values are mean (standard error) rating from +3 (strongly support) to -3 (strongly oppose). **Bold** values and those with different superscripts are significantly different ($p \leq 0.05$). n = 291-941.

Table 40. Support for within-wilderness zoning; use level variation.

Percent selecting the following regarding within-wilderness zoning	Very high	High	Moderate	All visitors	Low use
Do not restrict use to manage for solitude anywhere, even if use is heavy.	18	15	15	17	21
Manage for solitude along a few wilderness trails. The number of people allowed to use these trails will be limited, but the majority of trails will have no use limits and may be heavily used.	46	42	43	55	50
Manage for solitude on most wilderness trails, by limiting the number of people using these trails. A few trails will have unrestricted use. Use levels will be high on these trails.	32	36	36	25	26
Manage for solitude everywhere in wilderness, even though this may mean that use will be restricted and people will be turned away.	4	7	6	3	3

Percentages are not significantly different (p ≤ 0.05). n = 121-658.

ing more places for solitude than those who filled out the mailback questionnaire.

Differences between day and overnight users were statistically significant (table 41), but not substantial. The proportion of people supporting one of the two zoning options did not vary significantly between day and overnight users. The primary difference was in support for managing a few trails for solitude (preferred by more day users) rather than managing most trails for solitude (preferred by more overnight users).

Questions exploring visitor opinions about among-wilderness zoning were prefaced with the statement "some wilderness areas are within an hour's drive of large cities like Seattle and Portland, while others are far from such cities." Respondents were then asked to indicate the extent to which they agreed or disagreed with how wilderness close to cities should differ from wilderness far from cities. Two items addressed appropriate environmental conditions and four items addressed appropriate recreation management. Overall, there was modest support for among-wilderness zoning (table 42). The only item that was *not* supported by a majority of respondents was the statement that "in wilderness areas close to cities, it is OK to have more wear and tear on the vegetation from recreation use than in remote wilderness." In contrast

Table 41. Support for within-wilderness zoning; day and overnight users.

Percent selecting the following regarding within-wilderness zoning	Day	Overnight
Do not restrict use to manage for solitude anywhere, even if use is heavy.	17	16
Manage for solitude along a few wilderness trails. The number of people allowed to use these trails will be limited, but the majority of trails will have no use limits and may be heavily used.	46	41
Manage for solitude on most wilderness trails, by limiting the number of people using these trails. A few trails will have unrestricted use. Use levels will be high on these trails.	31	39
Manage for solitude everywhere in wilderness, even though this may mean that use will be restricted and people will be turned away.	6	4

Percentages are significantly different (p ≤ 0.05). n = 450-885.

Table 42. Support for among-wilderness zoning; use level variation.

In Wilderness Areas that are close to large cities like Seattle and Portland:	Very high	High	Moderate	All visitors	Low use
It is OK to see more people than in remote wildernesses	1.5(.05)	1.5(.07)	1.5(.07)	1.5(.06)	1.3(.14)
It is OK to have more wear and tear on the vegetation from recreation use than in remote wilderness	0.0(.07)	-0.2(.09)	-0.2(.10)	-0.1(.09)	-0.3(.16)
Managers should allow people to visit wilderness whenever they want, so they can get relief from the city	1.2(.06)	1.1(.08)	1.0(.09)	0.6(.08)	0.4(.16)
Use limits are more likely to be needed	0.8(.06)[a]	1.1(.08)[b]	1.1(.09)[b]	1.0(.07)	1.1(.14)
The behavior of visitors should be more tightly restricted	0.6(.06)[a]	0.8(.08)[a]	0.9(.08)[b]	0.7(.08)	0.9(.13)
It is more acceptable to manipulate the environment so it can withstand recreational use	0.4(.07)	0.4(.08)	0.4(.10)	0.5(.08)	0.5(.16)

Values are mean (standard error) rating from +3 (strongly support) to -3 (strongly oppose). Values with different superscripts are significantly different ($p \leq 0.05$). n = 115-622.

to lack of support for more lenient biophysical impact standards in urban-proximate wilderness, there was strong support for more lenient crowding-related standards in urban-proximate wilderness. Only 7 percent of respondents disagreed with the statement that "in wilderness areas that are close to cities, it is OK to see more people than in remote wildernesses."

About two-thirds of respondents supported allowing people to visit wilderness whenever they want in urban-proximate wilderness "so they can get relief from the city." A similar proportion agreed that use limits are more likely to be needed in urban-proximate wilderness. Interpreted strictly, these results are not logically consistent. This inconsistency likely reflects the personal values conflict many wilderness users feel about wanting access to wilderness to get away from the city and recognizing the need for limits. Alternatively, people could be responding to the "use limits" question by thinking about the future—as population continues to increase, use limits might ultimately be needed, especially to protect biophysical resources. Taken together, most respondents seem to believe that crowding standards should be more lenient in urban-proximate wilderness, resulting in an increased opportunity for people to visit these wildernesses when they want to, but also to believe that even with more lenient standards, use limits are still more likely in these wildernesses. Majorities also support more behavioral restrictions in urban-proximate wilderness and more environmental manipulation.

As was the case with support for within-wilderness zoning, support for among-wilderness zoning did not vary substantially with amount of use. Visitors exiting very heavy use trails were significantly less supportive of more behavioral restrictions in urban-proximate wilderness and less likely to agree that use limits are needed in urban-proximate wilderness (table 42). But differences were small. Low use visitor support was not significantly different from all visitor support for any of the among-wilderness questions.

Finally, day users were significantly more likely than overnight users to agree that people should be allowed to visit urban-proximate wilderness whenever they want (table 43). Day users were also more likely to agree that it is OK to see more people in urban-proximate wilderness.

Opinions Regarding Use Limits

We asked visitors whether they felt use limits were currently needed in the wilderness they visited by prefacing the reasons for limits with "if a limit is enforced your opportunity to visit may be reduced in the future." Then we explored the potential reasons for limiting use, asking visitors which they would support. We asked visitors about their preference for use limits or behavioral restrictions that deal with solving the problems of "too many people" and "too much recreation impact." Finally, we asked about their preference for use limits versus specific actions that might be taken instead.

Less than 20 percent of visitors believed that a use limit should be implemented at that time in the wilderness where they were contacted (table 44). As has been found in most other studies where this question has been asked, the most common response was that "no limit is needed now, but a limit should be imposed in the future when overuse occurs." Close to 40 percent of respondents stated that "there should never be a limit on use." Support for use limits did not vary significantly with use level. Though surprising, this result

Table 43. Support for among-wilderness zoning; day and overnight users.

In Wilderness Areas that are close to large cities like Seattle and Portland:	Day	Overnight
It is OK to see more people than in remote wildernesses	**1.6**(.04)	**1.3**(.07)
It is OK to have more wear and tear on the vegetation from recreation use than in remote wilderness	-0.1(.06)	-0.2(.08)
Managers should allow people to visit wilderness whenever they want, so they can get relief from the city	**1.2**(.05)	**1.0**(.07)
Use limits are more likely to be needed	0.9(.05)	0.9(.07)
The behavior of visitors should be more tightly restricted	0.7(.05)	0.7(.07)
It is more acceptable to manipulate the environment so it can withstand recreational use	0.4(.06)	0.4(.08)

Values are mean (standard error) rating from +3 (strongly support) to -3 (strongly oppose). **Bold** values are significantly different (p ≤ 0.05). n = 458-848.

Table 44. Opinions about the need to limit visitor use, now or in the future.

Percent selecting the following regarding use limits	Very high	High	Moderate	Day	Overnight
	------Percent------				
There should never be a limit on use	42	33	37	**40**	**35**
No limit is needed now, but should be imposed in the future when overuse occurs	41	49	46	**45**	**45**
A limit is needed now to hold use at the current level	13	13	13	**11**	**16**
A limit is needed now to lower use	5	5	3	**4**	**5**

Percentages differed significantly (p ≤ 0.05) between day and overnight users but not among use levels. n = 295-847.

might reflect different reasons for lack of support on low and high use trails. Support for use limits might be low in the less popular places because they are not highly crowded. Alternatively, support might be low in the very high use places because visitors feel high use is established and thus acceptable. Regardless, there was little support for use limits, even on the most crowded wilderness trails in the region. While 45 percent of visitors maintained that they would support limits *if* overuse occurred, it is not clear what criteria most visitors would use to define overuse. These very high use trails are already among the most crowded places in wilderness. Additionally, overnight users were more likely than day users to support limits, but differences were not pronounced (table 44).

We asked people who support limits now—or would in the future—to describe conditions that would indicate a need for limits. The response format was open-ended. As has often been reported, more people find physical impacts to be a compelling reason for limits versus social conditions. In order, the most frequently mentioned reasons were:

- ecological impact (mentioned by 44 percent of those who do or would support use limits)
- trail conditions (mentioned by 20 percent)
- litter (mentioned by 17 percent)
- crowding (mentioned by 16 percent)
- stock use (mentioned by 8 percent)
- off-trail areas disturbed (mentioned by 7 percent)
- wildlife (mentioned by 6 percent)
- dogs (mentioned by 5 percent)
- human waste (mentioned by 5 percent)
- campfires (mentioned by 3 percent)

There are many problems that might be reduced by limiting wilderness use. We solicited visitor opinions about which use limit reasons seemed most justified to them. We began by stating "the Forest Service wants to avoid limiting use in wilderness except where it is absolutely necessary." Then we asked people to consider each of 11 different reasons to limit use and to indicate how strongly they supported or opposed use limits as a means of solving

Table 45. Support for various reasons to limit use; use level variation.

I support limiting use in order to:	Very high	High	Moderate	All visitors	Low use
Avoid seeing lots of people	-0.4(.06)	-0.2(.08)	-0.2(.09)	0.1(.08)	-0.1(.15)
Avoid the need for frequent, intensive maintenance of trails and campsites	0.1(.06)	0.2(.08)	0.1(.09)	**0.3**(.08)	**-0.1**(.16)
Avoid the need to think about how your behavior affects other people	-0.8(.06)	-0.7(.08)	-0.7(.09)	-1.0(.08)	-1.2(.13)
Avoid impact on wildlife	1.3(.06)	1.4(.07)	1.3(.09)	**1.5**(.07)	**1.0**(.15)
Avoid having to worry about what other people are doing	-0.6(.06)	-0.4(.08)	-0.4(.09)	**-0.5**(.08)	**-0.9**(.14)
Avoid having to deal with inconsiderate people	-0.3(.07)	-0.1(.09)	-0.1(.10)	**0.0**(.09)	**-0.5**(.16)
Avoid a need for primitive toilets in the wilderness	**-0.3**(.07)[ab]	**-0.0**(.09)[a]	**-0.4**(.09)[b]	-0.3(.09)	-0.3(.16)
Avoid lots of evidence of previous visitors	**0.4**(.07)[a]	**0.7**(.08)[b]	**0.5**(.09)[ab]	0.6(.08)	0.3(.15)
Maintain the freedom to go and stop anywhere you want	0.0(.07)	0.1(.08)	-0.0(.10)	0.1(.08)	-0.1(.15)
Avoid impacts to soil and vegetation	1.3(.06)	1.4(.08)	1.2(.09)	1.5(.07)	1.3(.15)
Avoid the need for costly maintenance of trails and campsites	0.2(.07)	0.2(.08)	0.1(.09)	**0.2**(.08)[a]	**-0.1**(.16)[b]

Values are mean (standard error) rating from +3 (strongly agree) to -3 (strongly disagree). **Bold** values and those with different superscripts are significantly different ($p \leq 0.05$). n = 121-608.

each problem. Again, the most prominent finding was that avoidance of ecological impact provided a more compelling rationale for limiting use than avoiding impacts to visitor experiences. Majorities supported limiting use to "avoid impact on wildlife," "avoid impacts to soil and vegetation," and "avoid lots of evidence of previous visitors" (table 45). Reasons that were opposed much more than supported were to "avoid seeing lots of people," "avoid the need to think about how your behavior affects other people," and "avoid having to worry about what other people are doing." Visitors were more ambivalent about the five remaining reasons.

Support varied little by use level (table 45). For five of these reasons, support for limits was significantly lower among low use visitors compared to all visitors, despite the fact that low use visitors had stricter encounter standards (table 36). Among visitors given the exit survey, there were statistically significant differences among use levels for two of the 11 reasons—to avoid lots of evidence of previous visitors and to avoid the need for toilets. For both reasons, the strongest support was from the intermediate user category. There were also statistically significant differences between day and overnight users on two of the 11 reasons—to avoid lots of evidence of previous visitors and to avoid seeing lots of people (table 46). Overnight users were more supportive than day users of limiting use to avoid evidence of others, and less opposed to limiting use to avoid seeing lots of people. In all cases, however, these differences were small.

When problems arise, managers can choose between limiting use or regulating the behavior of visitors. We asked visitors for their opinion about how the Forest Service should respond to situations where "most visitors say they see too many other people in this wilderness." We gave visitors five options: two options to do nothing and options that emphasize use limits, emphasize behavioral regulations, and give equal emphasis to limits and regulations. Responses did not vary significantly with use level (table 47), but they did differ between those given the exit survey and those given a mailback questionnaire.

Among exiting visitors, the most common response was that the Forest Service should do nothing because "freedom from restriction is more important to the wilderness experience than not seeing other people." The least common response was to do nothing because "the number of people I see is not a very important issue." This suggests that, for those opposed to restriction, the number of people may be a salient issue, but freedom is more important. For the slight majority that felt that something should be done, there was substantial support for all three options, but behavioral restriction was somewhat preferred. Among those surveyed at home, support for doing something because of "too many people" was substantially greater (table 47). The most preferred option was equal emphasis on use limitation and behavioral restriction.

Table 46. Support for various reasons to limit use; day and overnight users.

I support limiting use in order to:	Day	Overnight
Avoid seeing lots of people	**-0.4**(.05)	**-0.2**(.08)
Avoid the need for frequent, intensive maintenance of trails and campsites	0.1(.05)	0.1(.07)
Avoid the need to think about how your behavior affects other people	-0.8(.05)	-0.7(.07)
Avoid impact on wildlife	1.3(.05)	1.2(.07)
Avoid having to worry about what other people are doing	-0.5(.06)	-0.4(.08)
Avoid having to deal with inconsiderate people	-0.2(.06)	-0.1(.08)
Avoid a need for primitive toilets in the wilderness	-0.3(.06)	-0.1(.08)
Avoid lots of evidence of previous visitors	**0.4**(.06)	**0.7**(.08)
Maintain the freedom to go and stop anywhere you want	0.0(.06)	0.1(.08)
Avoid impacts to soil and vegetation	1.3(.05)	1.2(.07)
Avoid the need for costly maintenance of trails and campsites	0.2(.06)	0.1(.08)

Values are mean (standard error) rating from +3 (strongly agree) to -3 (strongly disagree). **Bold** values are significantly different ($p \leq 0.05$). n = 452-829.

Table 47. Opinions about what the Forest Service should do in situations where most visitors say that they see too many other people in the wilderness; use level variation.

If visitors "see too many other people," the FS should: (select one)	Very high	High	Moderate	All visitors	Low use
	------------------Percent------------------				
Do nothing—the number of people I see is not a very important issue	8	8	7	6	8
Do nothing—freedom from restriction is more important to the wilderness experience than not seeing many people	40	35	38	19	25
Limit the number of people but place few regulations on people once they are inside the wilderness	13	15	17	12	12
Regulate activities within wilderness in order to avoid limiting use	22	24	19	28	21
Give equal emphasis to limiting use and regulating behavior	16	18	19	34	34

Percentages did not differ significantly among use levels ($p \leq 0.05$). n = 114-629.

The responses of day and overnight users did vary significantly (table 48), but support for action was similar. The primary difference was that the preference among day users for behavioral restriction was absent among overnight visitors.

We asked a similar question for situations where a "wilderness is so popular that most visitors say there is too much recreation impact" (damage to vegetation and soil). Once again, when the concern is ecological impact, visitors were much more supportive of restrictions. Again, differences among use levels were not statistically significant, but exiting visitors were less supportive of restriction than people surveyed at home (table 49). Of the exiting visitors, fewer than 20 percent supported "doing nothing" when the issue was ecological impact compared to about 45 percent who supported "doing nothing" when the problem was seeing too many other people. Of those surveyed at home, fewer than 10 percent supported "doing nothing" when the issue was ecological impact compared to about 20 percent who supported "doing nothing" when the problem was seeing too many other people. Although there was some support for relying primarily on limiting use, there was much more support for behavioral restriction or a combination of use limitation and behavioral restriction. There was little variation between visitor use levels. Finally, day users were significantly more supportive of regulation than overnight users, particularly behavioral restrictions (table 50).

Table 48. Opinions about what the Forest Service should do in situations where most visitors say that they see too many other people in the wilderness; day and overnight users.

If visitors "see too many other people," the FS should: (select one)	Day	Overnight
	-----Percent-----	
Do nothing—the number of people I see is not a very important issue	8	9
Do nothing—freedom from restriction is more important to the wilderness experience than not seeing many people	39	36
Limit the number of people but place few regulations on people once they are inside the wilderness	13	18
Regulate activities within wilderness in order to avoid limiting use	24	18
Give equal emphasis to limiting use and regulating behavior	17	19

*Percentages are significantly different (p ≤ 0.05). n = 461-844.

Table 49. Opinions about what the Forest Service should do in situations where most visitors say there is too much impact from recreation; use level variation.

If visitors say there is too much recreation impact, the FS should: (select one)	Very high	High	Moderate	All visitors	Low use
		----Percent----			
Do nothing—amount of recreation impact is not a very important issue	3	3	2	1	0
Do nothing—freedom from restriction is more important to the wilderness experience than avoiding recreation impact	18	15	14	6	15
Limit the number of people but place few regulations on people once they are inside the wilderness	16	18	20	10	8
Regulate activities within wilderness in order to avoid limiting use	41	38	40	39	30
Give equal emphasis to limiting use and regulating behavior	23	26	24	44	46

Percentages were not significantly different (p ≤ 0.05). n = 112-636.

We asked visitors about eight alternatives to use limits as a means of dealing with "management problems." Although it may not be true, we told them that these other actions would be as effective as use limits in dealing with problems. Six of the eight actions—outhouses, bulletin boards, ranger patrols, volunteer stewards, campsite closures, and campfire prohibitions—were strongly preferred over use limits (table 51). Use limits were strongly preferred to fishing prohibition and opinions were split regarding use limits or designated campsites. Surprisingly, a substantial proportion of visitors (over one-third) preferred use limits to "frequent ranger patrols to enforce regulations at popular destinations."

There was little difference among use levels (table 51). For none of these actions were the opinions of low use visitors significantly different from those of all visitors. Visitors to very high use places had significantly greater preference for issuing permits for designated campsites. This may reflect the greater proportion of day users in very high use places, as this action primarily affects overnight users. Indeed, for six of the eight actions, day users were significantly more likely than overnight users to prefer the action to use limits (table 52). Clearly, use limits seem even more onerous to day users than to overnight users.

Opinions About the Forest Service

Finally, we were interested in what visitors generally thought about the Forest Service and how well it was carrying out its wilderness stewardship role. We presented eight statements related to trust, management attention, and management appropriateness and asked visitors the extent to which they agreed or disagreed with each statement. They also had the option

Table 50. Opinions about what the Forest Service should do in situations where most visitors say there is too much impact from recreation; day and overnight users.

If visitors say there is too much recreation impact, the FS should: (select one)	Day	Overnight
	-------Percent-------	
Do nothing—amount of recreation impact is not a very important issue	2	4
Do nothing—freedom from restriction is more important to the wilderness experience than avoiding recreation impact	15	19
Limit the number of people but place few regulations on people once they are inside the wilderness	15	21
Regulate activities within wilderness in order to avoid limiting use	44	31
Give equal emphasis to limiting use and regulating behavior	23	26

Percentages were significantly different (p ≤ 0.05). n = 460-851.

Table 51. Percent of respondents preferring various management actions to limiting use, assuming both are equally effective; use level variation.

As an alternative to use limits, I prefer:	Very high	High	Moderate	All visitors	Low use
	--------------------Percent--------------------				
Outhouses at popular destinations	71	64	69	77	77
Bulletin boards with information on how to behave at popular destinations	79	79	76	76	75
Frequent ranger patrols to enforce regulations at popular destinations	65	61	66	66	71
Patrols by volunteer stewards at popular destinations	75	72	76	80	78
Prohibitions of fishing	40	38	38	49	48
Issuing permits so visitors may only camp in area/campsite assigned to them	55[a]	46[b]	43[b]	59	57
Closing portions of area to use so it can be restored	76	71	69	74	75
Prohibitions on campfires	**65**	**58**	**58**	**66**	**56**

Bold values and those with different superscripts were significantly different (p ≤ 0.05). n = 121-613.

Table 52. Percent of respondents preferring various management actions to limiting use, assuming both are equally effective; day and overnight users.

As an alternative to use limits, I prefer:	Day	Overnight
	-----Percent-----	
Outhouses at popular destinations	71	62
Bulletin boards with information on how to behave at popular destinations	81	73
Frequent ranger patrols to enforce regulations at popular destinations	66	60
Patrols by volunteer stewards at popular destinations	77	69
Prohibitions of fishing	37	42
Issuing permits so visitors may only camp in area/campsite assigned to them	**57**	**35**
Closing portions of area to use so it can be restored	75	69
Prohibitions on campfires	62	59

Bold values were significantly different (p ≤ 0.05). n = 429-837.

of "don't know." Most visitors volunteered opinions, although at least 30 percent responded that they "don't know" to the statements "the Forest Service often chooses wilderness management actions that are not effective" and "the Forest Service takes the Wilderness Act too literally when managing wilderness."

Most visitors trusted the Forest Service to manage wilderness appropriately and felt that it gives wilderness the management attention that it deserves (table 53). They did not think the Forest Service was too restrictive and they disagreed with the statement that "the Forest Service does not give sufficient consideration to wilderness visitors' needs and wants when creating restrictions." These opinions were positive, but they were also weak. Very few people felt strongly about Forest Service management. The strongest opinions about Forest Service management related to the inappropriateness of using motorized equipment (chainsaws and helicopters). Most people supported avoiding use of motorized equipment in wilderness, even if it would save money.

Opinions did not vary much with visitor use level (table 53). Among exiting visitors, none of the opinions differed significantly between use levels. Among respondents to the mailback survey, visitors to low use trails were somewhat less supportive of Forest Service management than all visitors. Low use visitors were significantly less likely to disagree that the Forest Service was "too restrictive," less likely to agree with the policy of not using motorized equipment, and less likely to disagree that "the Forest Service takes the Wilderness Act too literally." Differences between day and overnight users were not significant (table 54).

Summary and Management Implications

Many of the characteristics of wilderness visitors and their trips that we found in this study of Forest Service administered wilderness in Oregon and Washington are similar to what has been reported elsewhere (Cole and others 1997; Hendee and Dawson 2002; Roggenbuck and Lucas 1987). Hiking was the dominant mode of travel. Travel with stock was virtually nonexistent at all but 10 of the 36 trailheads and amounted to more than 5 percent of use at only three of the trailheads. Most visitors traveled short distances to the trailhead (50 percent lived within 100 miles) and took short trips. Two-thirds of visitors were on day trips and 44 percent of those on overnight trips were only out for one night. About one-fifth of the wilderness visitors reported that they only make day trips into wilderness. Groups were typically small. Groups of two were most common and less than three percent of groups contained more than ten people.

Table 53. Opinions about Forest Service wilderness management; use level variation.

	Very high	High	Moderate	All visitors	Low use
The Forest Service gives wilderness the management attention that it deserves	0.5(.07)	0.4(.09)	0.3(.10)	0.1(.09)	0.2(.15)
The Forest Service is too restrictive in its management of wilderness	-0.8(.06)	-0.9(.08)	-0.9(.09)	**-0.9**(.08)	**-0.5**(.15)
The Forest Service often chooses wilderness management actions that are not effective	0.1(.06)	0.2(.08)	0.2(.10)	0.2(.08)	0.5(.14)
The Forest Service should use motorized equipment (such as chainsaws and helicopters) more, if it would save money	-1.0(.08)	-0.8(.10)	-0.9(.11)	-0.5(.10)	-0.3(.21)
I trust the Forest Service to manage wilderness appropriately	0.4(.07)	0.3(.09)	0.3(.10)	0.1(.09)	-0.1(.16)
The Forest Service does not give sufficient consideration to wilderness visitors' needs and wants when creating restrictions	-0.5(.06)	-0.6(.08)	-0.5(.09)	-0.6(.07)	-0.4(.13)
I support the Forest Service's policy of not using motorized equipment (such as chainsaws and helicopters) in wilderness unless absolutely necessary	1.6(.07)	1.5(.09)	1.5(.10)	**1.4**(.09)	**0.9**(.20)
The Forest Service takes the Wilderness Act too literally when managing wilderness	-0.8(.07)	-0.9(.09)	-0.9(.11)	**-1.1**(.09)	**-0.5**(.20)

Values are mean (standard error) rating from +3 (strongly agree) to -3 (strongly disagree). **Bold** values were significantly different ($p \leq 0.05$). n = 91-501.

Table 54. Opinions about Forest Service wilderness management; day and overnight users.

	Day	Overnight
The Forest Service gives wilderness the management attention that it deserves	0.5(.06)	0.4(.09)
I trust the Forest Service to manage wilderness appropriately	0.4(.06)	0.2(.09)
The Forest Service often chooses wilderness management actions that are not effective	0.1(.05)	0.2(.08)
The Forest Service does not give sufficient consideration to wilderness visitors' needs and wants when creating restrictions	-0.6(.05)	-0.5(.07)
The Forest Service is too restrictive in its management of wilderness	-0.8(.05)	-0.8(.08)
The Forest Service takes the Wilderness Act too literally when managing wilderness	-0.8(.06)	-1.0(.09)
I support the Forest Service's policy of not using motorized equipment (such as chainsaws and helicopters) in wilderness unless absolutely necessary	1.5(.06)	1.6(.08)
The Forest Service should use motorized equipment (such as chainsaws and helicopters) more, if it would save money	-0.9(.07)	-1.1(.09)

Values are mean (standard error) rating from +3 (strongly agree) to -3 (strongly disagree). Values were not significantly different ($p \leq 0.05$). n = 357-718.

As had been found in earlier studies (Cole and others 1997), most visitors appeared to be highly satisfied with their trip and with wilderness conditions. Most reported that what they experienced on their trip was in line with their expectations, even in very heavily used places. Most people reported that they had the types of experiences that they desired. When asked to evaluate the severity of a number of potential problems, mean ratings were always low—between "not a problem" and "a slight problem." Many people did not notice problematic conditions in the first place.

When asked specifically about solitude, only 5 percent of visitors reported that solitude was important to them on their trip but they were unable to find it. About 50 percent of visitors reported that they found solitude and, for the rest, solitude was either unimportant or unexpected on the trip. Most visitors reported that they can have "a real wilderness experience" without having "a profound sense of solitude" or that they can have a profound sense of solitude "even if there are many other groups of people around." More people reported that the number of people they encountered added to their enjoyment than detracted from it, even in very high use places.

Encounters did detract from visitors' sense of being "in wilderness" and their "sense of solitude," but the vast majority of respondents considered any adverse effects to be small. In the most densely used places, the typical user encountered about 10 other groups during the day and estimated being in sight of other people about 30 percent of the time. These conditions do not appear to create high enough levels of crowding to be perceived as very problematic. When asked about the specific adverse effect of other groups, the most pronounced problem was the effect of others on "freedom from disruptions and distractions." But even in the most popular places, this problem had a mean rating of only 1.3 on a scale from 0 (no effect) to 6 (great effect).

Most visitors trusted the Forest Service to manage wilderness appropriately, believed that the Forest Service gives wilderness the management attention that it deserves, and felt that the Forest Service is not too restrictive in its management approach. There was little support for use limitation, particularly to deal with crowding-related problems. More people supported behavioral regulation as a visitor management strategy than limitation of use. Most people were more supportive of restrictions—even use limitation—as a means of avoiding biophysical impact versus problems with crowding and lack of solitude.

Differences Related to Amount of Use

Results of prior research on the relationship between use density and visitor experiences have often been equivocal (see reviews by Cole 2001a; Kuss and others 1990; Manning 1999). For example, among Colorado River boaters, Shelby (1980) found no relationship between number of encounters and satisfaction. Stronger relationships between encounters and crowding (r^2 as high as 0.36) have been found on heavily-used rivers (Hammitt and others 1984; Heberlein and Vaske 1977; Tarrant and others 1997) but not in wilderness-like settings. However, some researchers (for example, Manning 1999; Shelby and Heberlein 1986) consider these findings misleading due to the generality of the dependent variables examined. They argue that we should only expect use levels to affect specific aspects of visitor experiences. They also argue that studies do not account for various mechanisms for coping with high use densities, particularly visitor displacement.

With visitor displacement, they argue, those visitors most sensitive to density are not even included in the sample.

In our study, we extended previous work on use density effects by studying a wider array of dependent variables. Moreover, instead of studying an individual wilderness or river, we studied sites spread across the Pacific Northwest, including low-use places that should appeal to people displaced from high-use places.

As has been found before, however, differences among visitors related to the amount of use on the trail they selected were surprisingly small. We had expected people who selected lightly-used trails to be more sensitive to social impacts because we reasoned that people who choose to go to very high use places are accepting of those conditions and crowding-sensitive people would choose to go elsewhere. We also suspected that low-use visitors might be more experienced wilderness travelers, more interested in a true wilderness experience, and more willing to accept regulation to protect those experiences.

Few of these expectations proved to be true. Visitors to very high use trailheads were generally as experienced as visitors to low use trailheads, as attached to wilderness, and as concerned about how wilderness is managed. They were looking for similar experiences and typically had trips that met their needs and evaluated their trips as enjoyable wilderness experiences. They were similar to most other visitors in their support for, or opposition to, various management actions and the types of management approaches they favor over alternatives.

There were a few statistically significant differences, which we break out below according to the trailhead survey and the mailback survey (because results of the two studies cannot be directly compared). In all cases, the magnitude of differences among use levels was small. Compared to moderate use trailheads, at very high use trailheads:

- There were more repeat visitors, more day visitors, and more visitors from close by.
- Day trips were typically of longer duration.
- More other groups were encountered and other groups were in sight more of the time.
- Fewer people mentioned solitude as a high point of their trip and more mentioned crowding as a low point.
- Visitors saw about the same number of people as expected, rather than fewer people than expected (as was the case in less popular places).

- Visitors were slightly less able to experience "being away from crowds of people," "solitude," "closeness to nature," "being away from the modern world," "freedom," "wilderness," "remoteness," "surroundings not impacted by people," and "learning about this place" and they also reported less interest in these experiences.
- More visitors reported that they can, in principle, have a profound sense of solitude even with many other people around, and fewer agreed that solitude was critical to a real wilderness experience.
- More visitors reported that solitude was either not important to them on this trip or that it was not expected, while fewer reported that solitude was important and they found it.
- Conversely, more visitors reported that the actual number of other groups they saw adversely affected their sense of being in wilderness as well as their ability to set their own pace, sit and be quiet, and be free from disruptions and distractions.
- People-related problems were more frequently noticed, but they were evaluated as being only slightly more severe and only for the problem of a large number of day users.
- When asked about preferences and standards with regard to encounters, more visitors reported that the number of encounters doesn't matter to them and, if it did, their preferences were higher and their standards were more lenient.
- More visitors reported displacement and more mentioned crowding as the main reason for displacement.
- More visitors were supportive of prohibiting campfires, requiring visitors to pack out their human waste, and constructing toilets.

Low use visitors differed from the norm even less than did very high use visitors. They were more interested in solitude and more able to find it, but they were less supportive of use limitations in order to protect experiences. Compared to all visitors, low use visitors:

- Take more overnight trips and have visited fewer other wilderness areas.
- Were more able to experience "being away from crowds of people," "solitude," and "remoteness," and they were more interested in these experiences.

- Have lower preferences for number of encounters and their standards for encounters were more stringent.
- Were less supportive of some of the reasons for use limitations and more likely to feel that the Forest Service was too restrictive and "took the Wilderness Act too literally."

In addition to identifying differences between visitors to trails with different use levels, we also related use and encounter densities to experiences. We found relationships that were statistically significant but weak. Our results were consistent with those of Stewart and Cole (2001) who studied Grand Canyon backpackers on multi-day trips. Because the number of groups encountered varied among days, they were able to assess, for each individual, the relationship between use density and experience. They concluded, as earlier studies have, that visitors vary in their sensitivity to amount of use. However, underlying this variability were several consistent responses. Most visitors are adversely affected by increasing amount of use. The magnitude of effect is small, however; large differences in amount of use result in small differences in what people experience and in their evaluations of the quality of those experiences.

Collectively, these differences suggest that visitors to high use trailheads have had to adjust their tolerance of other wilderness users more than other visitors. Most knew of conditions they were likely to find and appeared to have adjusted their expectations accordingly. Consequently, their trip met most of their perceived needs and desires and, therefore, was enjoyable. They often adjusted the timing of their visits to avoid heavy use. Although they often encountered more other groups than they preferred, most people reported that they were still able to find solitude or at least have what they considered a real wilderness experience. This led most of them to oppose use limits for experience-related reasons, be more likely to report that "number of encounters doesn't matter to me," and be less likely to support a very stringent encounter standard.

Visitors to low-use trailheads were not very different from those who visit popular places. Including them in our mailback survey did not lead us to conclusions that differed from those of the trailhead survey in terms of the effect of amount of use on experience. Low-use visitors are distinguished as much by their interest in freedom from restriction as in their interest in getting away from others. This may at least partially explain why they too generally oppose limiting use in order to protect experiences.

Differences Between Day and Overnight Users

Differences between day and overnight visitors were also rather small, a finding similar to what has been reported elsewhere (Cole 2001b). There were some statistically significant differences, however. Compared to overnight users, day users:

- Were typically older and more likely to be female.
- Were more likely to be repeat visitors and to make more wilderness visits per year.
- Were more likely to be hiking by themselves.
- Were less likely to notice resource and social problems or to consider problems to be serious.
- Were more likely to mention solitude or wilderness as high points of their trip but more likely to note that there were no low points.
- Felt less strongly about most of the experiences they were seeking on their visit. Consequently, for a number of experiences ("to be away from crowds of people," "solitude," "a feeling of remoteness," and "a sense that the surroundings haven't been impacted by people"), what they actually experienced was more in line with what they hoped to experience.
- Considered solitude to be less important and were more likely to say that, in principle, they can experience solitude with many other people around.
- Were less adversely affected by other groups in less popular places but more adversely affected in the very high use places.
- Had higher preferences for number of encounters.
- When asked about standards for a maximum number of encounters, were more likely to report that the number of encounters doesn't matter to them and, if it did, their standards were more lenient.
- Were more supportive of a wide variety of management actions than overnight visitors, but they were even less supportive of use limits and had an even stronger preference for behavioral restriction, as opposed to use limitation, as a visitor management approach.

Many of these characteristics of day users are similar to characteristics of visitors to very high use trailheads. In part, this reflects the fact that day use is disproportionately high at very high use trailheads. To a substantial degree, the unique issues at the very high use trailheads are largely about day use. However, day users everywhere also appeared to be generally more tolerant than overnight users, particularly of crowding (Cole 2001b). Their needs and desires, regarding experiences, were somewhat less pronounced and, therefore, more easily met. They often had more limited expectations, particularly regarding the ability to get away from crowds at a popular trailhead. Day users appeared to have even more ability than overnight users to adjust to high use densities through rationalizations about solitude not being important or not expected or by finding ways to experience solitude even with many other people around.

Methodological Implications

Survey-based visitor studies usually employ either on-site or mailback questionnaires. Because we used both in this study, we were able to assess whether each approach yields the same findings. Compared to the on-site results, mailback results suggested that visitors have higher motivations, lower experience achievement and, consequently, less ability to have the experiences they wanted. They appeared more interested in solitude, more concerned about number of encounters, and more likely to have stringent encounter standards. Consistent with this, they were more supportive of behavioral restrictions but not of use limits. In our study, results from the mailback instrument differed from the on-site instrument for confounding reasons: (1) only permit holders were surveyed and (2) respondents had to remember back to their wilderness experiences in total. Observed differences might reflect either the responses of more experienced group leaders or a tendency to become more idealistic in one's opinions when at home—far removed from the actual wilderness experience—and when generalizing across all wilderness trips.

Indicators and Standards

Our results provide some insight into potential indicators and standards that might guide recreation management in wilderness. Most visitors clearly thought that keeping biophysical impacts to acceptable levels was critically important everywhere in wilderness. They did not support allowing substantial impact even in wildernesses close to large cities (table 42) and were willing to support use limits for the purpose of avoiding excessive impact (tables 45 and 49). At moderate use trailheads in particular, biophysical impact problems, specifically those caused by packstock, were judged more severe than people problems (table 20). In addition, the desired experience that was least achieved was having a sense of the surroundings not being impacted by people (table 24). This suggests that indicators of biophysical impact are particularly important. In Denali National Park, Lawson and Manning (2002) also found that concern about resource conditions was most important to wilderness visitors. However, it is important to note that there is often little congruence between visitor abhorrence of the idea of biophysical impact and their obliviousness to the reality of the impacts actually encountered in wilderness. In places with high levels of impact, many visitors do not notice it; few consider it highly problematic and it seldom influences their choices of where to visit or camp (Cole and others 1997; White and others 2001).

People-related problems were judged to be somewhat more severe by visitors to the very high use trailheads (table 20). Moreover, at those trailheads, the ability to be away from crowds of people was the desired experience that was least achieved (table 24). When asked specifically what it was about the number of other people that had the greatest adverse effect on their experience, "freedom from disruptions and distractions" was the most common response (table 32). This suggests that, while managers may still want to use number of encounters with other groups as an indicator, it might be helpful to consider number of encounters to be a proxy for a concern with people being disturbed and interrupted. Freedom from disruption and distraction increases as number of encounters decreases, everything else being equal. Consequently, by limiting encounters, we increase freedom from disruption and distraction. If managers choose to retain encounters as an indicator, they must recognize that the relationship between number of reported encounters and freedom from distraction and disruption is weak. Limiting encounters will have a positive effect but the effect will be small.

Responses regarding zoning suggest that most visitors supported variable standards, with some trails allowed to be more crowded than others and wildernesses close to large cities allowed to be more densely used than more remote wildernesses. What is less clear is what appropriate standards should be for different wilderness zones. The questions we asked about encounter preferences and evaluative standards provide insight into the opinions of current visitors. While some researchers suggest that such data provide a strong empirical foundation for the formulation of standards (Manning 2007; Shelby and others 1996), we are less enthusiastic. We are concerned about the difference in response between visitors exiting the wilderness and visitors responding to a mailback questionnaire some time after their trip. For example, 32 percent of those contacted at the trailhead reported that the number of other groups they see doesn't matter to them, compared to only 16 percent of those contacted at home. It is not clear whether precedence should be given to immediate opinions or those obtained after a time of reflection. Caution is also warranted given the wide range of responses about appropriate standards and given the bimodal distribution in which the most common responses are either to allow unlimited encounters or limit encounters to rather low levels. What these data illustrate is the need for managers to make difficult decisions about both the type of visitor whose opinions matter most and the types of experience to be provided.

Despite these concerns, our data can be used to gain insight into the opinions of various types of users. For example, managers may want to manage for the median user. For very high use trailheads, the median user preferred to encounter 10 groups per day (table 55). Encounters started to detract from the experience at 20 groups per day, and when they reached 50 groups per day, the median user reported that they would rather not visit. At high use trailheads, median users preferred encountering five groups per day; encounters started to detract at 10 encounters per day; and median users reported they would be displaced at 20 encounters per day. Moderate use trailheads were not very different from high use trailheads. Visitors to low use trailheads, however, were quite different. Median users preferred two groups per day; encounters started to detract at four encounters per day; and users thought they would be displaced at 10 encounters per day.

Alternatively, managers might want to manage for visitors who are substantially less tolerant of crowding than the median visitor, for example, someone at the 25th percentile on these scales. For very high use trailheads, such a user preferred to encounter four groups per day. Encounters started to detract from the experience at 10 groups per day, and when they reached 20 groups per day, this less tolerant user reported that they would rather not visit. At the other extreme, at low use trailheads, such a user preferred to encounter just one group per day; encounters started to detract at three encounters per day; and users thought they would be displaced at five encounters per day.

Similarly, it would be possible to focus on the opinions of substantially more tolerant visitors than the norm (the 75th percentile). Their standards were even higher (less stringent) than those presented for the median user. In fact, at the very high visitor use

Table 55. Encounter preferences and evaluative standards of different visitor types from trailheads with different use levels[a].

	Use type		
	Encounter intolerant	**Median user**	**Encounter tolerant**
Very High Use			
Preference	4	10	∞
Begins to detract	10	20	∞
Would displace	20	50	∞
High Use			
Preference	3	5	∞
Begins to detract	5	10	∞
Would displace	10	20	∞
Moderate Use			
Preference	2	5	20
Begins to detract	5	10	20
Would displace	10	15	80
Low Use			
Preference	1	2	4
Begins to detract	3	4	10
Would displace	5	10	25

[a] Values are encounters with other groups per day. For visitors who responded that encounters do not matter, it was assumed that their standards for encounters per day were at the high end of the range of possible values (∞). In addition to the median respondent, results are provided for visitors that are relatively intolerant of encounters (25th percentile) and visitors who are relatively tolerant (75th percentile).

and high use trailheads, these people do not care about encounters—suggesting a standard of unlimited encounters.

This discussion highlights the difficult choices managers face when attempting to use this so-called normative information to set standards. As table 55 indicates, managers can develop an empirical rationale for virtually any standard they might want to select, from one group per day to an unlimited number of encounters. They must decide, for any specific place in wilderness, which user they are managing for and what conditions they are trying to provide. Whatever is decided, certain groups will be pleased, and others will be displeased.

Despite this need to select a particular user type to favor in any specific place, it is possible to meet the needs of a broader array of stakeholders by making different decisions in different places. A diversity of conditions can be provided through zoning, an approach that most respondents endorsed. Some lands could be managed to meet the needs of those visitors least tolerant of encounters by having standards as low as two encounters per day or less. Twenty-three percent of visitors exiting at trailheads (and 39 percent of those given mailback surveys) preferred seeing two other groups per day or less. Some other lands could be managed with a standard in the range of five to 10 groups per day. This would appeal to a large portion of those currently selecting moderate use trailheads. Beyond this, decisions are more difficult. There are clearly numerous advocates for placing no limits on encounters if it would limit access. This preference could be accommodated by having certain zones with no standards for encounters. Use may still need to be limited in such places but the purpose of limits would be to control biophysical impacts, not crowding. Or perhaps, these preferences should not be accommodated. Perhaps there is also a need for zones in which encounters are limited to 25-30 groups per day. This is an encounter level at which large portions of people, even in more heavily used places, reported that their experience is beginning to be significantly degraded.

Appropriate Management Actions

The overwhelming conclusion regarding management actions is that most visitors did not support limiting use in order to protect solitude, provide more freedom, or to avoid the need for behavioral restrictions. They supported use limitations to limit impact to vegetation, soil, and animals, but not to limit encounters with other people. Most visitors trusted the Forest Service and supported its general management approach. There was strong support for avoiding the use of motorized equipment, even if it would save money. Where necessary, majorities supported such actions as posting information about appropriate behavior on signs on bulletin boards (even inside the wilderness), posting directional signs, prohibiting campfires, and confining camping to designated sites. Limiting overnight use was not opposed to the degree that limiting day use was.

Overall, this study suggests that there are problems resulting from very high use of some wilderness lands in Oregon and Washington because high use reduces opportunities for solitude and other desired experiences. However, it is clear that from most visitors' point of view, these problems are not very substantial. Most visitors recognized that they were seeing more people than they preferred—more than would be ideal in wilderness. However, most visitors concluded that this is a small price to pay for open access. Most visitors found that these densely used places still offered enjoyable experiences that met their needs, desires, and expectations—experiences that they still considered to be "a real wilderness experience." Consequently, most visitors did not support use limitation as a means of avoiding people-related problems. For most, the solution to crowding problems was much more costly than the problem itself.

This conclusion contrasts with that of some researchers who have reported that there is considerable support for use rationing and allocation (Manning 2007). Some evidence for support comes when visitors are asked hypothetically about their support for the concept of use limits. Indeed, in our study, a majority of respondents supported limiting use in theory. But even those who had just encountered 50 groups of people or more were most likely to say that limits are needed *if* overuse occurs, but not now. This raises the question of whether there would ever be a point where use would be so high that such people would support a use limit. Most of the support for the conclusion that visitors support use limitation comes from studies of visitors in places where use limits are already in place (for example, Stankey 1979). This is a useful finding but it may reflect displacement of users who are intolerant of restrictions, as was found by Hall and Cole (2000) in a study of newly-applied use limits.

Finally, our conclusion that there is little support for use limits, under current circumstances, is based on the opinions of the majority of wilderness visitors. It is important to remember that there is a minority of visitors with opposing views. Some visitors reported that other visitors adversely affected them to a great degree, solitude was critical to their wilderness experience and they could not find it, and they thought use limits were needed to lower use. These opinions were held by about five percent of the visitors we surveyed. Managers could still decide that it is most appropriate to manage wilderness to meet the needs of these people. Alternatively, they could try to base management policies on their perceptions of legal and agency mandates, regardless of the opinions of the majority of visitors.

References

Chavez, Deborah J. 2000. Wilderness visitors in the 21st century: diversity, day-use, perceptions, and preferences. International Journal of Wilderness 6(2): 10-11.

Cole, David N. 2001a. Visitor use density and wilderness experiences: a historical review of research In: Freimund, Wayne A.; Cole, David N., comps. Visitor use density and wilderness experience: proceedings; 2000 June 1-3: Missoula, MT. Proceedings RMRS-P-20. Ogden, UT: U.S. Department of Agriculture, Forest Service, Rocky Mountain Research Station: 11-20.

Cole, David N. 2001b. Day users in wilderness: how different are they? Research Paper RMRS-RP-31. Ogden, UT: U.S. Department of Agriculture, Forest Service, Rocky Mountain Research Station. 29 p.

Cole, David N.; Watson, Alan E.; Hall, Troy E.; Spildie, David R. 1997. High-use destinations in wilderness: social and biophysical impacts, visitor responses, and management options. Research Paper INT-RP-496. Ogden, UT: U.S. Department of Agriculture, Forest Service, Rocky Mountain Research Station. 30 p.

Glaspell, Brian; Watson, Alan; Kneeshaw, Katie; Pendergrast, Don. 2003. Selecting indicators and understanding their role in wilderness experience stewardship at Gates of the Arctic National Park and Preserve. The George Wright Forum 20(3): 59-71.

Haas, Glenn; Wells, Marcella. 2000. A more pristine wilderness. International Journal of Wilderness 6(2): 21-22.

Hall, Troy E. 2001. Hikers' perspectives on solitude and wilderness. International Journal of Wilderness 7(2): 20-24.

Hall, Troy E.; Cole, David N. 2000. An expanded perspective on displacement: A longitudinal study of visitors to two wildernesses in the Cascade Mountains of Oregon. In: McCool, S.F., Cole, D.N.; Borrie, W.T.; O'Loughlin, J. eds. Wilderness science in a time of change conference—Volume 4: Wilderness visitors, experiences and visitor management. 1999 May 23-27. Proceedings RMRS-P-15-VOL-4. Ogden, UT: U.S. Department of Agriculture, Forest Service, Rocky Mountain Research Station: 113-121.

Hammitt, William E.; McDonald, Cary D.; Noe, Frank P. 1984. Use level and encounters: important variables of perceived crowding among nonspecialized recreationists. Journal of Leisure Research 16:1-8.

Heberlein, Thomas A.; Vaske, Jerry J. 1977. Crowding and visitor conflict on the Bois Brule River. Report WISC WRC77-04. Madison, WI: University of Wisconsin, Water Resources Center. 100 p.

Hendee, John C.; Dawson, Chad P. 2002. Wilderness management: stewardship and protection of resources and values, 3rd ed. Fulcrum Publishing, Golden, CO. 640 p.

Kuss, Fred R.; Graefe, Alan R.; Vaske, Jerry J. 1990. Visitor impact management: a review of research. Washington, DC: National Parks and Conservation Association. 256 p.

Lawson, Steven R.; Manning, Robert E. 2002. Tradeoffs among social, resource, and managerial attributes of the Denali wilderness experience: a contextual approach to normative research. Leisure Sciences 24: 297-312.

Manning, Robert E. 1999. Studies in outdoor recreation: search and research for satisfaction, 2nd ed. Oregon State University Press, Corvallis, OR. 374 p.

Manning, Robert E. 2007. Parks and carrying capacity: commons without tragedy. Washington, DC: Island Press. 313 p.

Papenfuse, Meghan K.; Roggenbuck, Joseph W.; Hall, Troy E. 2000. The rise of the day visitor in wilderness: should managers be concerned? In: McCool, S.F., Cole, D.N.; Borrie, W.T.; O'Loughlin, J. eds. Wilderness science in a time of change conference—Volume 4: Wilderness visitors, experiences and visitor management. 1999 May 23-27. Proceedings RMRS-P-15-VOL-4. Ogden, UT: U.S. Department of Agriculture, Forest Service, Rocky Mountain Research Station: 148-154.

Roggenbuck, Joseph W.; Lucas, Robert C. 1987. Wilderness use and user characteristics: a state-of-knowledge review. In: Lucas, R.C., comp. Proceedings—national wilderness research conference: issues, state-of-knowledge, future directions. 1985 July 23-26. General Technical Report INT-220. Ogden, UT: U.S. Department of Agriculture, Forest Service, Intermountain Research Station: 204-245.

Salant, Priscilla; Dillman, Don A. 1994. How to conduct your own survey. New York, NY: John Wiley Company. 232 p.

Seekamp, Erin; Hall, Troy; Harris, Chuck; Cole, David. 2006. Attitudes and changes in attitudes about visitor management at the Green Lakes/South Sister area of the Three Sisters Wilderness: a study of four stakeholder involvement meetings in Oregon. 71 p. Unpublished paper available online at: http://leopold.wilderness net/research/fprojects/docs7/Stakeholder.pdf.

Shelby, Bo. 1980. Crowding models for backcountry recreation. Land Economics 56: 43-55.

Shelby, Bo; Heberlein, Thomas A. 1986. Carrying capacity in recreation settings. Corvallis, OR: Oregon State University. 164 p.

Shelby, Bo; Vaske, Jerry J.; Donnelly, M. 1996. Norms, standards and natural resources. Leisure Sciences 18: 103-123.

Spring, Ira. 2001. If we lock people out, who will fight to save wilderness? International Journal of Wilderness 7(1): 17-19.

Stankey, George H. 1979. Use rationing in two southern California wildernesses. Journal of Forestry 77: 347-349.

Stewart, William P.; Cole, David N. 2001. Number of encounters and experience quality in Grand Canyon backcountry: consistently negative and weak relationships. Journal of Leisure Research 33: 106-120.

Tarrant, Michael A.; Cordell, H. Kenneth; Kibler, Tamela L. 1997. Measuring perceived crowding for high-density river recreation: the effects of situational conditions and personal factors. Leisure Sciences 19: 97-112.

Watson, Alan E.; Roggenbuck, Joseph W. 1997. Selecting human experience indicators for wilderness: different approaches provide different results. In: Kulhavy, D.L.; Legg, M.H., eds. Wilderness and natural areas in eastern North America: research, management and planning. Nacogdoches, TX: Stephen F. Austin State University, Center for Applied Study in Forestry: 264-269.

White, Dave D.; Hall, Troy E.; Farrell, Tracy A. 2001. Influence of ecological impacts and other campsite characteristics on wilderness visitors' campsite choices. Journal of Park and Recreation Administration 19: 83-97.

Worf, Bill. 2001. The new Forest Service wilderness recreation strategy spells doom for the National Wilderness Preservation System. International Journal of Wilderness 7(1): 15-16.

APPENDIX A:.

Trailhead Exit Questionnaire Version 1

Section 1: Trip Characteristics

1.1 How long was your trip? (Mark one.)

☐ Overnight. How many nights total did you spend in the wilderness? _____

☐ Day trip. How many hours did you spend in the wilderness? _____

1.2 How many people (including yourself) are in your group? _____

1.3 What was your primary destination on this trip? _____

1.4 What were the **high** points of your trip—the best experiences—and why?

	High point:	What made it so good?
1		
2		
3		

1.5 What were the **low** points of your trip—the worst experiences—and why?

	Low point:	What made it so bad?
1		
2		
3		

USDA Forest Service RMRS-RP-71. 2008.

Section 2: Your Motivations for Taking This Trip

2.1 The following are feelings or experiences that people sometimes seek in wilderness. For each, please indicate how much you hoped to get it from this trip AND how much you actually got it on this trip. (Circle **two** numbers for each item.)

	How much were you *seeking* it? Not at all — Very much	How much did you *experience* it? Not at all — Very much
A sense of freedom	1 2 3 4 5 6 7	1 2 3 4 5 6 7
Solitude	1 2 3 4 5 6 7	1 2 3 4 5 6 7
To think about who I am	1 2 3 4 5 6 7	1 2 3 4 5 6 7
Closeness to nature	1 2 3 4 5 6 7	1 2 3 4 5 6 7
To learn about this place	1 2 3 4 5 6 7	1 2 3 4 5 6 7
Wilderness opportunities	1 2 3 4 5 6 7	1 2 3 4 5 6 7
A feeling of remoteness	1 2 3 4 5 6 7	1 2 3 4 5 6 7
A sense that the surroundings haven't been impacted by people	1 2 3 4 5 6 7	1 2 3 4 5 6 7
To be away from crowds of people	1 2 3 4 5 6 7	1 2 3 4 5 6 7
A sense of challenge	1 2 3 4 5 6 7	1 2 3 4 5 6 7
A sense of being away from the modern world	1 2 3 4 5 6 7	1 2 3 4 5 6 7
To be near others who could help if I need them	1 2 3 4 5 6 7	1 2 3 4 5 6 7
To be my own boss	1 2 3 4 5 6 7	1 2 3 4 5 6 7
To develop personal, spiritual values	1 2 3 4 5 6 7	1 2 3 4 5 6 7

2.2 Please check **one** of the responses below to indicate how important a sense of solitude was to you on this visit.
- ○ A sense of solitude was not important to me on this visit.
- ○ I hoped to find solitude, but did not expect it on this visit.
- ○ Solitude was important to me on this visit, and I found it.
- ○ Solitude was important to me on this visit, but I didn't find it.

2.3 We are interested in your preferences regarding encounters with other groups in this area.
A. Ideally, how many other groups per day would you **want** to see in this wilderness? (Mark one.)
- ☐ The number of other groups I see doesn't matter to me.
- ○ My preference for the number of groups to see per day is: _____

B. Ideally, what percent of time would you **want** to be in sight of other people in this wilderness? (Mark one.)
- ☐ The percent of time I see other groups doesn't matter to me.
- ○ My preference for the percent of time in sight of other groups is: (Circle a number)

0---5---10---15---20---25---30---35---40---45---50---55---60---65---70---75---80---85---90---95---100%

Section 3: Visitor Characteristics and Past Experience

3.1 Have you ever been to a wilderness before this trip?
○ No. (*Skip to Section 4*) →
☐ Yes.

3.2 Since your first wilderness trip, about how often have you gone on wilderness trips (including this and other wildernesses)? (Mark one.)
☐ Less than once every 2 years
☐ Less than once a year
☐ Once a year
☐ 2-5 times a year
☐ 6-10 times a year
☐ More than 10 times a year

3.3 How many times have you been to **this destination or area** before?
○ Never. (First trip.)
☐ 1-2
☐ 3-5
☐ 6-10
☐ 11-20
☐ More than 20

3.4 About what percent of your **wilderness trips** (either here or elsewhere) during a typical year are **overnight** trips? (Make a mark on the scale below.)

0---5---10---15---20---25---30---35---40---45---50---55---60---65---70---75---80---85---90---95---100%

3.5 About how many **other** wilderness areas, besides this wilderness, have you visited?
○ None
☐ 1-5
☐ 6-10
☐ 11-15
☐ 16-20
☐ More than 20

3.6 We are interested in how the other wilderness areas you have visited compare with this place. How many of the other wilderness areas you have visited...

How many wildernesses...	Almost All of them	Most of them (at least 50%)	Some of them (less than 50%)	None of them
Had fewer people	☐	☐	☐	☐
Had less evidence of human use	☐	☐	☐	☐
Had less evidence of management activity	☐	☐	☐	☐

3.7 Please indicate the extent to which you agree or disagree with each of the following statements about the importance of wilderness to you personally.

	Strongly agree	Agree	Neutral		Disagree	Strongly disagree
I find that a lot of my life is organized around wilderness use	+3	+2	+1	0	-1	-2	-3
I feel like wilderness is a part of me	+3	+2	+1	0	-1	-2	-3
I get greater satisfaction out of visiting wilderness than other areas	+3	+2	+1	0	-1	-2	-3

Section 4: Things You Experienced on This Trip

4.1 About how many other groups did you see today? (Make a mark on the line.)

   0   2   4   6   8   10   12   14   16   18   20   22   24   26   28   30   32   34   36   38   40   >40

4.2 About what percent of the time were you in sight of other groups of visitors today? _____ %

4.3 Did you camp last night?
   ◯ No. (*Skip to Question 4.8*)
   ☐ Yes

4.4 Where did you camp last night? _____

4.5 How many other groups were camped within sight or sound of you? _____

4.6 On a **typical** day during your trip, about how many groups did you see?

   0—2—4—6—8—10—12—14—16—18—20—22—24—26—28—30—32—34—36—38—40→40

4.7 On the day you saw the **fewest** other people, about how many groups did you see?

   0—2—4—6—8—10—12—14—16—18—20—22—24—26—28—30—32—34—36—38—40→40

4.8 Please indicate the extent to which you were adversely affected by the other groups you encountered on this trip.

How much did other groups adversely affect your:	Not at all		Slightly		Moderately		Greatly
Ability to set your own pace along the trail	0	1	2	3	4	5	6
Choice of where to do the things you wanted to do (camp, picnic, fish, swim, etc.)	0	1	2	3	4	5	6
Ability to sit and be quiet	0	1	2	3	4	5	6
Freedom from disruptions or distractions	0	1	2	3	4	5	6
Freedom to behave as you wanted	0	1	2	3	4	5	6
Freedom to decide with whom to interact	0	1	2	3	4	5	6

4.9 How did the **number** of groups you saw during this trip add to or detract from each of the following aspects of your experience?

	Encounters added		No Effect	Encounters detracted	
	A Lot	A Little		A Little	A Lot
My enjoyment	+3	+2	+1	0	-1	-2	-3
My sense I was in Wilderness	+3	+2	+1	0	-1	-2	-3
My sense of solitude	+3	+2	+1	0	-1	-2	-3
My sense of freedom	+3	+2	+1	0	-1	-2	-3

4.10 At what point does the number of other groups that you encounter in the wilderness **begin to detract** from your experience, if at all? (Mark one)

☐ The number of other groups I see doesn't matter to me.
◯ It would begin to bother me if I saw more than about _____ groups per day.

4.11 The following characteristics of recreational areas can influence the quality of a trip. For each, please indicate how they affected your wilderness experience **on this trip**. If you did not notice an item, circle "nn."

	Not Noticed	How much of a problem was it?						
		Not at all		Slight		Moderate		Big
Noisy groups	nn	1	2	3	4	5	6	7
Large numbers of day users	nn	1	2	3	4	5	6	7
Trail wear and tear	nn	1	2	3	4	5	6	7
Rules that restrict where people can camp	nn	1	2	3	4	5	6	7
Trampled areas where people have camped or walked	nn	1	2	3	4	5	6	7
Large groups	nn	1	2	3	4	5	6	7
Trails that are poorly marked	nn	1	2	3	4	5	6	7
Inconsiderate behavior by other visitors	nn	1	2	3	4	5	6	7
Large numbers of overnight users	nn	1	2	3	4	5	6	7
Area rules/regulations not adequately enforced	nn	1	2	3	4	5	6	7
Litter left behind by visitors	nn	1	2	3	4	5	6	7
Too many rules or regulations	nn	1	2	3	4	5	6	7
Human waste	nn	1	2	3	4	5	6	7
Contact with a wilderness ranger or volunteer	nn	1	2	3	4	5	6	7
Having to fill out a permit or registration form	nn	1	2	3	4	5	6	7
Organized groups or outfitted parties	nn	1	2	3	4	5	6	7
Impacts from recreational packstock	nn	1	2	3	4	5	6	7
Uncontrolled dogs	nn	1	2	3	4	5	6	7
Concern about your personal security	nn	1	2	3	4	5	6	7

4.12 On this trip, how did the following compare with what you **expected** in the wilderness?

	Compared to what I expected, the number or amount was:					
	Far Less	Less	About What I Expected		More	Far More
The number of people you saw	-3	-2	-1	0	+1	+2	+3
Evidence of impact from human use	-3	-2	-1	0	+1	+2	+3
Rules and regulations	-3	-2	-1	0	+1	+2	+3

4.13 At what point does the number of other groups that you encounter **detract so much from your experience that you would not come here**? (Mark one.)

☐ The number of other groups I see doesn't matter to me.

○ I would not come here if I knew I would see more than about _____ groups per day

Section 5: Some Information about You.

5.1 How familiar are you with the legal definition of Wilderness?
- ○ I have no idea – I didn't even know there was a land classification of "Wilderness."
- ○ I have heard of Wilderness areas, but I don't know anything about the specific definition.
- ○ I know a little bit about what legally classified Wilderness is.
- ○ I think I know a lot about the legal definition of Wilderness.

5.2 What is your age? _____

5.3 Approximately how many miles (one-way) do you live from this wilderness? _____.

5.4 What is your zip code? _____

5.5 Are you ___ male or ___ female?

APPENDIX B:

Questions Asked on the Other Three Versions of the Trailhead Exit Questionnaires But Not on Version 1

From Questionnaire Version 2

3.7 We are interested in how important solitude is to your conception of what a wilderness experience should be. Thinking about **wilderness experience generally** (not just this visit) please indicate the extent to which you agree or disagree with each of the following statements.

	Strongly agree	Agree		Neutral		Disagree	Strongly disagree
I cannot have a real wilderness experience unless I have a profound sense of solitude	+3	+2	+1	0	-1	-2	-3
Solitude adds to the wilderness experience, but is not critical	+3	+2	+1	0	-1	-2	-3
I can have a profound sense of solitude in wilderness, even if there are many other groups of people around	+3	+2	+1	0	-1	-2	-3
I cannot have a profound sense of solitude unless there are no other groups of people around	+3	+2	+1	0	-1	-2	-3
I cannot have a profound sense of solitude unless I am completely alone	+3	+2	+1	0	-1	-2	-3

5.1 The following are policies or actions the Forest Service could take to protect the wilderness. Please indicate how much you support or oppose each one for **this** wilderness.

	Strongly Support			Neutral		Strongly Oppose	
Install information about proper behavior on bulletin boards within the area	+3	+2	+1	0	-1	-2	-3
Construct toilets in the area	+3	+2	+1	0	-1	-2	-3
Limit the number of day users	+3	+2	+1	0	-1	-2	-3
Limit the number of overnight users	+3	+2	+1	0	-1	-2	-3
Post directional trail signs	+3	+2	+1	0	-1	-2	-3
Prohibit campfires	+3	+2	+1	0	-1	-2	-3
Require people to pack out their human waste	+3	+2	+1	0	-1	-2	-3
Prohibit dogs	+3	+2	+1	0	-1	-2	-3
Require camping at designated sites	+3	+2	+1	0	-1	-2	-3

From Exit Questionnaire Version 3

Section 5: Your Decisions about Where to Go in Wilderness

5.1 Have you ever intentionally avoided trails or places in **THIS wilderness** for any reason?
○ No.
☐ Yes. Where? _____
For what reason(s)
_____

5.2 Have you ever decided not to visit **THIS wilderness** because of the **amount of use**?
○ No
☐ Yes.

5.3 Are there **other wilderness** areas that have places or times that you avoid because of the amount of use?
○ No.
☐ Yes. What wilderness(es)? _____

Section 6: Your Attitudes toward Management of THIS Area

6.1 How important to you personally is the way this area is managed? (Check one.)

☐ Not at all—I've never really thought about it.
○ Not very—I haven't given it much thought and am not very concerned.
○ Somewhat—I haven't thought a lot about it, but it seems important.
○ Very—I think about it sometimes and have some concerns.
○ Extremely—I think about it a lot and am very concerned.
○ I don't know.

6.2 Forest Service managers must find an appropriate balance between allowing all people to visit the wilderness when they want and providing opportunities for solitude. In your opinion, which of the four following options strikes the best balance for **this wilderness**? (Circle one letter.)

A. *Do not restrict use to manage for solitude* anywhere, even if use is heavy.

B. Manage for *solitude along a few wilderness trails*. The number of people allowed to use these few trails will be limited, but the majority of trails will have no use limits and may be heavily used.

C. Manage for *solitude on most wilderness trails*, by limiting the number of people using these trails. A few trails will have unrestricted use. Use levels will be high on these trails.

D. Manage for *solitude everywhere* in wilderness, even though this may mean that use will be restricted and people will be turned away.

6.3 If you could change the management of this place in any way, what would you change?

Section 7: Your Attitudes toward Management of Wilderness in General

7.1 Please indicate your level of agreement or disagreement with each of the following statements about Forest Service wilderness management. If you do not know, circle "DK".

	Don't Know	Strongly Agree			No Opinion		Strongly Disagree	
The Forest Service gives wilderness the management attention that it deserves.	DK	+3	+2	+1	0	-1	-2	-3
The Forest Service is too restrictive in its management of wilderness.	DK	+3	+2	+1	0	-1	-2	-3
The Forest Service often chooses wilderness management actions that are not effective.	DK	+3	+2	+1	0	-1	-2	-3
The Forest Service should use motorized equipment (such as chain saws and helicopters) more in wilderness, if it would save money.	DK	+3	+2	+1	0	-1	-2	-3
I trust the Forest Service to manage wilderness appropriately.	DK	+3	+2	+1	0	-1	-2	-3
The Forest Service does not give sufficient consideration to wilderness visitors' needs and wants when creating restrictions.	DK	+3	+2	+1	0	-1	-2	-3
I support the Forest Service's policy of not using motorized equipment (such as chain saws and helicopters) in wilderness unless absolutely necessary.	DK	+3	+2	+1	0	-1	-2	-3
The Forest Service takes the Wilderness Act too literally when managing wilderness.	DK	+3	+2	+1	0	-1	-2	-3

7.2 Often management problems can be lessened EITHER by limiting the number of people OR by doing something else. Below are pairs of actions that would be equally effective at solving certain problems. Please indicate which you prefer within each pair, by checking either the action or "use limits."

Action:

Action		
☐ Outhouses at popular destinations	OR	☐ use limits
☐ Bulletin boards, with information on how to behave, at popular destinations	OR	☐ use limits
☐ Frequent ranger patrols to enforce regulations at popular destinations	OR	☐ use limits
☐ Patrols by volunteer stewards at popular destinations	OR	☐ use limits
☐ Prohibitions on fishing	OR	☐ use limits
☐ Issuing permits so visitors may only camp in an area or campsite assigned to them	OR	☐ use limits
☐ Closing portions of the area to use so it can be restored	OR	☐ use limits
☐ Prohibitions on campfires	OR	☐ use limits

From Exit Questionnaire Version 4

Section 5: Your Attitudes toward Management of THIS Area

5.2 If most visitors say they see too many other people in this wilderness, what (if anything) do you think the Forest Service should do? (Check one.)

☐ Nothing—the number of people I see is not a very important issue.

○ Nothing—freedom from restriction is more important to the wilderness experience than not seeing many other people.

○ The Forest Service should limit the number of people but place few regulations on people once they are inside the wilderness.

○ The Forest Service should regulate activities within wilderness (such as campsite restrictions, one-way trails, prohibitions on dogs, designated picnic areas, etc.) in order to avoid limiting use.

○ The Forest Service should give equal emphasis to limiting use AND regulating behavior.

5.3 If this wilderness is so popular that most visitors say there is too much recreation impact (damage to vegetation and soil), what (if anything) do you think the Forest Service should do? (Check one.)

☐ Nothing—amount of recreation impact is not a very important issue.

○ Nothing—freedom from restriction is more important to the wilderness experience than avoiding recreation impact.

○ The Forest Service should limit the number of people but place few regulations on people once they are inside the wilderness.

○ The Forest Service should regulate activities within wilderness (such as campsite restrictions, one-way trails, prohibitions on dogs, designated picnic areas, etc.) in order to avoid limiting use.

○ The Forest Service should give equal emphasis to limiting use AND regulating behavior.

5.4 Do you feel a limit is needed on the number of people using this wilderness, recognizing that if a limit is enforced your own opportunity to visit may be reduced in the future? (Mark one.)

☐ No, there should never be a limit on the number of people using the area.

○ No limit is needed now, but should be imposed in the future when overuse occurs.

○ Yes, a limit is needed now to HOLD use at the current level.

○ Yes, a limit is needed to LOWER the current level of use.

If you checked one of these three circles, please describe the kinds of conditions that indicate a need for limits:

Section 6: Your Attitudes toward Management of Wilderness in General

6.1 Some wilderness areas are within an hour's drive of large cities like Seattle and Portland, while others are far from such cities. Please indicate whether you agree or disagree with the following statements about how wilderness areas close to cities should differ from remote wilderness areas.

	Strongly agree	Agree	Neutral		Disagree	Strongly disagree	
In Wilderness Areas that are **close** to cities, it is OK to see more people than in remote wildernesses.	+3	+2	+1	0	-1	-2	-3
In Wilderness Areas that are **close** to cities, managers should allow people to visit wilderness whenever they want, so they can get relief from the city.	+3	+2	+1	0	-1	-2	-3
In Wilderness Areas that are **close** to cities, it is OK to have more wear and tear on the vegetation from recreation use than in remote wilderness.	+3	+2	+1	0	-1	-2	-3
In Wilderness Areas that are **close** to cities, the behavior of visitors should be more tightly restricted.	+3	+2	+1	0	-1	-2	-3
In Wilderness Areas that are **close** to cities, it is more acceptable to manipulate the environment so it can withstand recreational use.	+3	+2	+1	0	-1	-2	-3
In Wilderness Areas that are **close** to cities, use limits are more likely to be needed.	+3	+2	+1	0	-1	-2	-3

6.2 The Forest Service wants to avoid limiting use in wilderness except where it is absolutely necessary. Consider each of the following potential reasons to limit use and indicate how much you would support or oppose use limits to solve each problem.

	Strongly agree	Agree	Neutral	Disagree	Strongly disagree		
Limit use to avoid seeing lots of other people.	+3	+2	+1	0	-1	-2	-3
Limit use to avoid the need for frequent, intensive maintenance of trails and campsites.	+3	+2	+1	0	-1	-2	-3
Limit use to avoid the need to think about how your behavior affects other people.	+3	+2	+1	0	-1	-2	-3
Limit use to avoid impact on wildlife.	+3	+2	+1	0	-1	-2	-3
Limit use to avoid having to worry about what other people are doing.	+3	+2	+1	0	-1	-2	-3
Limit use to avoid having to deal with inconsiderate people.	+3	+2	+1	0	-1	-2	-3
Limit use to avoid a need for primitive toilets in the wilderness.	+3	+2	+1	0	-1	-2	-3
Limit use to avoid lots of evidence of previous visitors.	+3	+2	+1	0	-1	-2	-3
Limit use to maintain the freedom to go and stop anywhere you want.	+3	+2	+1	0	-1	-2	-3
Limit use to avoid impacts to soil and vegetation.	+3	+2	+1	0	-1	-2	-3
Limit use to avoid the need for costly maintenance of trails and campsites.	+3	+2	+1	0	-1	-2	-3

APPENDIX C:

Mailback Questionnaire

(several items on the questionnaire were deleted because results are not reported here)

Section 1: Visitor Characteristics and Past Experience

1.1 Since your first wilderness trip, about how often have you gone on wilderness trips? (Mark one.)

☐ Less than once every 2 years ☐ 2-5 times a year
☐ Less than once a year ☐ 6-10 times a year
☐ Once a year ☐ More than 10 times a year

1.2 About what percent of your **wilderness trips** during a typical year are **overnight** trips? (Make a mark on the scale below.)

0---5---10---15---20---25---30---35---40---45---50---55---60---65---70---75---80---85---90---95---100%

1.3 About how many different **Congressionally-designated** wilderness areas have you visited?

○ None ☐ 6-10 ☐ 16-20
☐ 1-5 ☐ 11-15 ☐ More than 20

4.4 Please indicate the extent to which you agree or disagree with each of the following statements about the importance of wilderness to you personally.

	Strongly agree	Agree	Neutral	Disagree	Strongly disagree		
I find that a lot of my life is organized around wilderness use	+3	+2	+1	0	-1	-2	-3
I feel like wilderness is a part of me	+3	+2	+1	0	-1	-2	-3
I get greater satisfaction out of visiting wilderness than other areas	+3	+2	+1	0	-1	-2	-3

1.5 How familiar are you with the legal definition of Wilderness? (Mark one.)

☐ I have no idea – I didn't even know there was a land classification of "Wilderness."
○ I have heard of Wilderness areas, but I don't know anything about the specific definition.
○ I know a little bit about what legally classified Wilderness is.
○ I think I know a lot about the legal definition of Wilderness.

Section 2: Your Motivations for Visiting Wilderness

2.1 The following are feelings or experiences that people sometimes seek in wilderness. For each, please indicate how important it typically is on your wilderness trips AND how often you experience it on wilderness trips. (Circle **two** numbers for each item.)

	How important is it? Not at all — Extremely	How often do you experience it? Never — Always
A sense of freedom	1 2 3 4 5 6 7	1 2 3 4 5 6 7
Solitude	1 2 3 4 5 6 7	1 2 3 4 5 6 7
To think about who I am	1 2 3 4 5 6 7	1 2 3 4 5 6 7
Closeness to nature	1 2 3 4 5 6 7	1 2 3 4 5 6 7
To learn about the place	1 2 3 4 5 6 7	1 2 3 4 5 6 7
Wilderness opportunities	1 2 3 4 5 6 7	1 2 3 4 5 6 7
A feeling of remoteness	1 2 3 4 5 6 7	1 2 3 4 5 6 7
A sense that the surroundings haven't been impacted by people	1 2 3 4 5 6 7	1 2 3 4 5 6 7
To be away from crowds of people	1 2 3 4 5 6 7	1 2 3 4 5 6 7
A sense of challenge	1 2 3 4 5 6 7	1 2 3 4 5 6 7
A sense of being away from the modern world	1 2 3 4 5 6 7	1 2 3 4 5 6 7
To be near others who could help if I need them	1 2 3 4 5 6 7	1 2 3 4 5 6 7
To be my own boss	1 2 3 4 5 6 7	1 2 3 4 5 6 7
To develop personal, spiritual values	1 2 3 4 5 6 7	1 2 3 4 5 6 7

Section 3: Solitude and Encounters with other People

3.1 We are interested in how important solitude is to your conception of what a wilderness experience should be. Thinking about **wilderness experience generally** please indicate the extent to which you agree or disagree with each of the following statements.

	Strongly agree	Agree	Neutral	Disagree	Strongly disagree		
I cannot have a real wilderness experience unless I have a profound sense of solitude	+3	+2	+1	0	-1	-2	-3
Solitude adds to the wilderness experience, but is not critical	+3	+2	+1	0	-1	-2	-3
I can have a profound sense of solitude in wilderness, even if there are many other groups of people around	+3	+2	+1	0	-1	-2	-3
I cannot have a profound sense of solitude unless there are no other groups of people around	+3	+2	+1	0	-1	-2	-3
I cannot have a profound sense of solitude unless I am completely alone	+3	+2	+1	0	-1	-2	-3

3.2 We are interested in your preferences regarding encounters with other groups when you visit a wilderness area.

    A. Ideally, how many other groups per day would you **want** to see? (Mark one.)

        ☐ The number of other groups I see doesn't matter to me (Skip to Section 4)

        ☐ My preference for the number of groups to see per day is: _____

    B. At what point does the number of other groups that you encounter **begin to detract** from your experience?

It would begin to bother me if I saw more than about _____ groups per day.

    C. At what point does the number of other groups that you encounter **detract so much from your experience that you would not visit the wilderness?**

I would not visit if I knew I would see more than about _____ groups per day.

Section 5: Your Attitudes about Wilderness Management

5.1 How important to you personally is the way that wilderness areas are managed? (Check one.)

- ☐ Not at all—I've never really thought about it.
- ○ Not very—I haven't given it much thought and am not very concerned.
- ○ Somewhat—I haven't thought a lot about it, but it seems important.
- ○ Very—I think about it sometimes and have some concerns.
- ○ Extremely—I think about it a lot and am very concerned.
- ○ I don't know.

5.3 Please indicate your level of agreement or disagreement with each of the following statements about Forest Service wilderness management. If you do not know, circle "DK".

	Don't Know	Strongly Agree			No Opinion			Strongly Disagree
The Forest Service gives wilderness the management attention that it deserves.	DK	+3	+2	+1	0	-1	-2	-3
The Forest Service is too restrictive in its management of wilderness.	DK	+3	+2	+1	0	-1	-2	-3
The Forest Service often chooses wilderness management actions that are not effective.	DK	+3	+2	+1	0	-1	-2	-3
The Forest Service should use motorized equipment (such as chain saws and helicopters) more in wilderness, if it would save money.	DK	+3	+2	+1	0	-1	-2	-3
I trust the Forest Service to manage wilderness appropriately.	DK	+3	+2	+1	0	-1	-2	-3
The Forest Service does not give sufficient consideration to wilderness visitors' needs and wants when creating restrictions.	DK	+3	+2	+1	0	-1	-2	-3
I support the Forest Service's policy of not using motorized equipment (such as chain saws and helicopters) in wilderness unless absolutely necessary.	DK	+3	+2	+1	0	-1	-2	-3
The Forest Service takes the Wilderness Act too literally when managing wilderness.	DK	+3	+2	+1	0	-1	-2	-3

5.4 Some wilderness areas are within an hour's drive of large cities like Seattle and Portland, while others are far from such cities. Please indicate whether you agree or disagree with the following statements about how wilderness areas close to cities should differ from remote wilderness areas.

	Strongly agree	Agree	Neutral		Disagree	Strongly disagree	
In Wilderness Areas that are **close** to cities, it is OK to see more people than in remote wildernesses.	+3	+2	+1	0	-1	-2	-3
In Wilderness Areas that are **close** to cities, managers should allow people to visit wilderness whenever they want, so they can get relief from the city.	+3	+2	+1	0	-1	-2	-3
In Wilderness Areas that are **close** to cities, it is OK to have more wear and tear on the vegetation from recreation use than in remote wilderness.	+3	+2	+1	0	-1	-2	-3
In Wilderness Areas that are **close** to cities, the behavior of visitors should be more tightly restricted.	+3	+2	+1	0	-1	-2	-3
In Wilderness Areas that are **close** to cities, it is more acceptable to manipulate the environment so it can withstand recreational use.	+3	+2	+1	0	-1	-2	-3
In Wilderness Areas that are **close** to cities, use limits are more likely to be needed.	+3	+2	+1	0	-1	-2	-3

5.5 If most visitors say they see too many other people in a wilderness, what (if anything) do you think the Forest Service should do? (Check one.)

☐ Nothing—the number of people I see is not a very important issue.
☐ Nothing—freedom from restriction is more important to the wilderness experience than not seeing many other people.
☐ The Forest Service should limit the number of people but place few regulations on people once they are inside the wilderness.
☐ The Forest Service should regulate activities within wilderness (such as campsite restrictions, one-way trails, prohibitions on dogs, designated picnic areas, etc.) in order to avoid limiting use.
☐ The Forest Service should give equal emphasis to limiting use AND regulating behavior.

5.6 If a wilderness is so popular that most visitors say there is too much recreation impact (damage to vegetation and soil), what (if anything) do you think the Forest Service should do? (Check one.)

- ☐ Nothing—amount of recreation impact is not a very important issue.
- ◯ Nothing—freedom from restriction is more important to the wilderness experience than avoiding recreation impact.
- ◯ The Forest Service should limit the number of people but place few regulations on people once they are inside the wilderness.
- ◯ The Forest Service should regulate activities within wilderness (such as campsite restrictions, one-way trails, prohibitions on dogs, designated picnic areas, etc.) in order to avoid limiting use.
- ◯ The Forest Service should give equal emphasis to limiting use AND regulating behavior.

Section 6: Some Information about You.

6.1 What is your age? _____

4.4 Are you ___ male or ___ female?

Do you have any other comments you would like to make?

APPENDIX D:
Questions Asked on the Other Version of the Mailback Questionnaires But Not on Version 1

Section 4: Your Attitudes about Wilderness Management

4.2 Forest Service managers must find an appropriate balance between allowing all people to visit the wilderness when they want and providing opportunities for solitude. In your opinion, which of the four following options strikes the best balance? (Circle one letter.)

A. *Do not restrict use to manage for solitude* anywhere, even if use is heavy.

B. Manage for *solitude along a few wilderness trails.* The number of people allowed to use these few trails will be limited, but the majority of trails will have no use limits and may be heavily used.

C. Manage for *solitude on most wilderness trails*, by limiting the number of people using these trails. A few trails will have unrestricted use. Use levels will be high on these trails.

D. Manage for *solitude everywhere* in wilderness, even though this may mean that use will be restricted and people will be turned away.

4.3 Often management problems can be lessened EITHER by limiting the number of people OR by doing something else. Below are pairs of actions that would be equally effective at solving certain problems. Please indicate which you prefer within each pair, by checking either the action or "use limits."

Action:

☐ Outhouses at popular destinations	OR	☐ use limits
☐ Bulletin boards, with information on how to behave, at popular destinations	OR	☐ use limits
☐ Frequent ranger patrols to enforce regulations at popular destinations	OR	☐ use limits
☐ Patrols by volunteer stewards at popular destinations	OR	☐ use limits
☐ Prohibitions on fishing	OR	☐ use limits
☐ Issuing permits so visitors may only camp in an area or campsite assigned to them	OR	☐ use limits
☐ Closing portions of the area to use so it can be restored	OR	☐ use limits
☐ Prohibitions on campfires	OR	☐ use limits

4.4 The Forest Service wants to avoid limiting use in wilderness except where it is absolutely necessary. Consider each of the following potential reasons to limit use and indicate how much you would support or oppose use limits to solve each problem.

	Strongly agree	Agree	Neutral	Disagree	Strongly disagree		
Limit use to avoid seeing lots of other people.	+3	+2	+1	0	-1	-2	-3
Limit use to avoid the need for frequent, intensive maintenance of trails and campsites.	+3	+2	+1	0	-1	-2	-3
Limit use to avoid the need to think about how your behavior affects other people.	+3	+2	+1	0	-1	-2	-3
Limit use to avoid impact on wildlife.	+3	+2	+1	0	-1	-2	-3
Limit use to avoid having to worry about what other people are doing.	+3	+2	+1	0	-1	-2	-3
Limit use to avoid having to deal with inconsiderate people.	+3	+2	+1	0	-1	-2	-3
Limit use to avoid a need for primitive toilets in the wilderness.	+3	+2	+1	0	-1	-2	-3
Limit use to avoid lots of evidence of previous visitors.	+3	+2	+1	0	-1	-2	-3
Limit use to maintain the freedom to go and stop anywhere you want.	+3	+2	+1	0	-1	-2	-3
Limit use to avoid impacts to soil and vegetation.	+3	+2	+1	0	-1	-2	-3
Limit use to avoid the need for costly maintenance of trails and campsites.	+3	+2	+1	0	-1	-2	-3

Made in the USA
Middletown, DE
29 July 2017